transcenDance

Also by Michael Bernard Beckwith

The Answer Is You
Heart-Sets & Mind-Sets for Self-Discovery

40-Day Mind Fast Soul Feast
A Guide to Soul Awakening and Inner Fulfillment

Life Visioning
A Transformative Process for Activating Your Unique Gifts and Highest Potential

Spiritual Liberation
Fulfilling Your Soul's Potential

Inspirations of the Heart
Artistic Expressions by F. Rassouli

A Manifesto of Peace

TranscenDance

MICHAEL
BERNARD
BECKWITH

Agape Media International

Published by Agape Media International, LLC
5700 Buckingham Parkway
Culver City, California 90230
310.258.4401 | www.agapeme.com

Distributed by Hay House, Inc.
P.O. Box 5100, Carlsbad, CA 92018-5100
760.431.7695 or 800.654.5126
www.hayhouse.com®

Hay House UK: www.hayhouse.co.uk
Hay House Australia: www.hayhouse.com.au
Hay House South Africa: www.hayhouse.co.za
Hay House India: www.hayhouse.co.in

TranscenDance Expanded
Michael Bernard Beckwith

Executive In Charge of Publication: Stephen Powers
Editor | Chapters 1–8: Kuwana Haulsey
Copy Editor & Editor | Chapter 9: Anita Rehker
Art Direction & Design: Benjamin Cziller | www.ImageDriven.com
Photography: Carl Studna | www.CarlStudna.com
Transcription Coordinator: Alissa Sanders
Transcriptions: Marion Lougheed

CD © ℗ 2012 Agape Media International, LLC
Book © 2012 Michael Bernard Beckwith

ISBN: 978-1-4019-4085-0

Printed in USA on recycled paper

Certified Chain of Custody
Promoting Sustainable Forestry
SUSTAINABLE FORESTRY INITIATIVE
www.sfiprogram.org
SFI-01268

SFI label applies to the text stock

AUDIO PRODUCTION

Featuring the words of
Michael Bernard Beckwith

Produced by **Stephen Bray** and **John Potoker**
Executive Producers: **Michael Bernard Beckwith**
  and **Stephen Powers**

Michael Bernard Beckwith lead vocals
Stephen Bray programming, keyboards
  (all tracks except 8)
John Potoker programming, keyboards (track 8)
Randy Emata additional keyboards (tracks 1, 2, 5, 6)
Philippe Saisse additional keyboards (tracks 2, 3, 8)
James Harrah guitars (tracks 1, 2, 4, 5)
Luis Conte percussion (tracks 1, 2)
Cynthia Bass backing vocals (tracks 2, 4)
Bridgette Bryant backing vocals (tracks 2, 4)
Brenda Lee Eager guest vocal (track 2),
  backing vocals (tracks 2, 4)
Siedah Garrett guest vocal (track 4)
Niki Haris guest vocal (track 3)
Sovory guest vocals (tracks 1, 5)
Wendi Williams backing vocals (track 2)

All songs written by Michael Bernard Beckwith and
  Stephen Bray

Recorded and mixed by **John Potoker** and
Stephen Bray for Soultone at Saturn Sound
and Direct Inject

Niki Haris's vocals recorded by Nigel Lawrence at
Nigel Maestro Productions

Michael Bernard Beckwith recorded live (except
track 9) at Agape International Spiritual Center
www.agapelive.com

Additional digital editing by Fil Brown
Mastered by Brian Gardner at Bernie Grundman
Mastering

Photography: Carl Studna, www.carlstudna.com

Art Direction & Design: Benjamin Cziller,
Image Driven Media Design, www.ImageDriven.com

TranscenDance began as a series of one-hour wisdom teachings by Michael Bernard Beckwith recorded live during weekly Sunday and Wednesday services at the Agape International Spiritual Center in Los Angeles.

Executive Producer Stephen Powers approached songwriter Stephen Bray in 2007 with the idea of a Beckwith dance music album. "The Rev"—as he is affectionately called—speaks in natural rhythm and rhyme, and Powers envisioned a collection designed to lift the listener into an ecstatic union of mind, body, and spirit. Selecting from hundreds of Beckwith recordings, he identified high-impact teachings communicated in uniquely compelling language, a task made easier by the richness and variety of Beckwith's monthly themes and weekly topics.

Bray began looking for phrases to encapsulate the teachings. Anyone who has attended Agape knows that Beckwith's inimitable musicality rises and falls in cadence with the vibratory energy of his delivery. As the project evolved, themes and topics became hooks and choruses. First verses were the perfect place to outline concepts such as *One Day in Heaven* and *Adventure in Paradise*. Second verses and bridges were ideal for expanding on universal principles and spiritual practices. Following months of meticulous editing, Beckwith's talks were gently nudged into the musical building blocks of a genre Michael and his wife, singer and composer Rickie Byars Beckwith, have coined as "Rhythm & Joy."

Co-producer and mix master John Potoker chose a classic Beckwith theme to energize *Life Is Good,* where over a thousand members of the Agape community can be heard loud and strong.

With song structures nine established, The Rev added vocal overdubs and spontaneous flow to sweeten the mix. Guest vocalists Siedah Garrett, Niki Haris, Brenda Lee Eager, and Sovory raised the vibration even higher with soaring melodies and soulful harmony. To complete the collection, Bray composed music for a guided meditation to be recorded "live" in the studio. Without script or notes, Michael listened "with the ear behind the ear" and allowed *Mystic Cord of Memory* to flow through in one continuous take. With the recorded material complete, several hundred hours in the expert hands of Potoker served to refine, polish, and mix the tracks for maximum impact.

The creative process came full circle with a book and CD set featuring complete transcriptions of the nine Beckwith talks transformed into songs. *TranscenDance Expanded* provides an opportunity to explore in-depth the nuanced, fully expressed teachings of Michael Bernard Beckwith.

A complete schedule of the original talks listed by their original titles (theme and topic) and the recording date of each is included herein.

Dig in. Breathe deep. Expand.

ORIGINAL TRANSCENDANCE TALKS BY MICHAEL BERNARD BECKWITH

1.   Adventure In Paradise

Theme: An Adventure In Paradise
Topic: Spiritual Stimulus Package
Date: Sunday, February 22, 2009

2.   Let It Be Alright

Theme: Star Power
Topic: Your God Light
Date: Sunday, December 2, 2007

3.   Who Loves You, Baby

Theme: From Mental Pollution
         To Spiritual Solution
Topic: Who Loves You, Baby
Date: Wednesday, July 29, 2009

4.   U R The Answer

Theme: Inspiration, Focus and Resolve:
         It's Time To Make A U-Turn
Topic: U U U Are The Answers!
Date: Sunday, October 11, 2009

5.   One Day In Heaven

Theme: Creatively Maladjusted
Topic: A Day In Heaven
Date: Wednesday, September 12, 2007

6.   In This Love Together (Part 1)

Theme: Creatively Maladjusted
Topic: Laying Up Treasures In Heaven
Date: Sunday, September 30, 2007

In This Love Together (Part 2)

Theme: A Good Crisis Is A Terrible
         Thing to Waste
Topic: Breakdown To Breakthrough
Date: Sunday, March 29, 2009

7.   Energetic Shapeshifter

Theme: Full Dimensional Living
Topic: Energetic Shapeshifting - Part III
Date: Sunday, July 15, 2007

8.   Life Is Good

Theme: The Art Of Letting Go
Topic: Prepare To Receive
Date: Sunday, March 28, 2010

CONTENTS

There is no point in time when the mysticism of music has not been a vital component in all of my creative expressions. Whether I am teaching spiritual growth classes, facilitating seminars, teaching in the school of ministry, conducting silent retreats, or writing books or lyrics to songs—all aspects of sadhana—the inspiration and healing elements, of music are integral to these endeavors. Since long ago, when I inwardly discovered that music is connected to the unfoldment of the soul, it has played a major role in my own transformational practices. It is no wonder that music has a significant place in the weekly celebrations, classes, and conferences of the Agape International Spiritual Center.

I have always especially encouraged spiritual seekers to be aware of the soundtrack within their own lives. For example, are they moving to a rhythm of victim songs or to anesthetize themselves from the challenging blows that come their way? Or are they living in cadence with the musical notes of inspiration, upliftment, triumph, and joy?

The package you hold in your hands includes a CD that falls into the genre of what Rickie BB and I call "rhythm and joy." The tracks you will be listening to are a combination of my teachings, which began as Sunday or Wednesday talks, blended with the music of Stephen Bray. The selections are more than spoken word or dance music; they are joyful soundtracks that have been created to inspire you to listen and dance to the beauty of your own true nature.

A debt of gratitude goes to Stephen Bray and John Potoker for their countless hours of mixing magic, to Stephen Powers for being a powerful glue assisting in pulling it all together, and to the singers who dropped by the studio to add their voices to the cosmic mix. And of course to the beloved community of Agape that, for 25 years now, has pulled the words that I speak from deep within my heart.

As you strike your Mystic "Chord" of Memory, here is something for your spiritual soundtrack.

Peace and Richest Blessings,

Michael Bernard Beckwith

Even though it has been 20 years since I first heard Rickie Byars sing *Use Me*, I can easily recall the profound mixture of emotion that nearly floored me. The sense of being at home both musically and spiritually was literally life changing. Spending the next 15 years playing the drums with Rickie's choir fulfilled my ulterior motive of steeping myself in the words of Beckwith and music of Byars. This project has allowed me to join two of my favorite things: dance music and the dynamic teachings of Michael Bernard Beckwith. I am grateful to have been given the opportunity to immerse myself in these transformational words while setting them to good vibrations. It is my hope that with *TranscenDance* you can get your Beckwith party started whenever and wherever you like!

- Stephen Bray

Photo: S.A. Bray

1   Adventure In Paradise

Your Divine stimulus package
Is activating the gifts of Divinity within you
That you may express them
You will express them beyond your wildest imagination
And joy, joy breaks out all over
It's the real source
Feel it! Feel it in your bones
Take a holy breath and say to yourself
I'm taking an adventure in paradise
And guess what? I'm taking you with me!

There's a spiritual love affair going on between yourself and all of life, which is happening on a different level than your personality. There are dimensions of your being interplaying with dimensions of other people's beings. The dance that's created by this spiritual play is a cause for tremendous glee. It's part of a universal celebration that's occurring at every moment.

We do our spiritual work/play so that can break out of the limiting confines of our minds, and begin to see what's happening everywhere in God's universe. When you participate fully in this celebration, you begin to recognize that you're not cut adrift or set apart from anyone else. Perhaps you may have gotten snagged as you made your way along this journey through time and space. But even so, you have the opportunity to open up to spirit and rebirth yourself.

Like being immersed into a Leboyer bath, you can allow your spiritual limbs to stretch out, and with no one looking, just fall in love with God. You can fall in love with yourself (who God is within), fall in love with each and every individual that you meet, and become aware that we're all here in this moment to participate in paradise.

Our journey through this life is an adventure in paradise, an adventure in eternity and ever-expanding good. It's an adventure in divine supply—as we move through the life experience, we have the opportunity to come onto the awareness that all of our needs are met. We can move ever deeper into the understanding that our steps are ordered by the Lord, the great law of life. When we surrender to the real nature of our being, which is harmonizing abundance and fulfillment, it becomes possible to wake up in our daily lives to the knowledge that we're fueled and financed by the presence of God in every area. We get to grow and glow from glory to greater glory, regardless of circumstance.

Perhaps you've bought into the old story that you have to go out into a fitful, cold, hard, cruel world and struggle to make your way. You might have been told that something wrong is out there, and someone else is to blame. Something is missing within you and you have to look outside of yourself to get it. Something is broken within you and you have to find a way to fix it. If you buy into this particular paradigm, you can spend your entire life struggling to get the things you need, do what's expected of you, and fix all the things that are supposedly wrong with you. However, the other alternative is to simply stand in the awareness that you're on an adventure in divine love, then watch as the universe bends back upon itself and rolls up at your feet, reflecting and revealing the cosmic order from which you emanate.

You are part of a spiritual stimulus package, fueled and financed by God. The economies of the world are fueled and funded by nonrenewable energy sources, thus having scarcity built into the system already. So, regardless of what you do to it, at some point these systems fail. They see-saw up and down. But your stimulus package begins with the awareness that you are sourced by God. You are sourced by beauty and love and joy, the ineffable qualities of the spirit. You are sourced by something that has no beginning and has no end.

You can vote to say yes to this stimulus package by saying yes to it in your heart. That *yes* carries with it the awareness that you already have everything you want, hope for, and desire. The renewable energy source that generates your good creates no pollution whatsoever. It's the presence of beauty and God and love in your soul.

There's an eternal broadcast happening that's so beautiful and magnificent that all of creation is screaming with it: "I am alive! I am here! I am now! I am available!" Life is in celebration of its connection with the great power and presence and love of spirit. This particular broadcast is emanating from within your own being. Heretofore, you may have thought God was speaking (if He spoke to you at all) from somewhere up in the sky. You may have believed that the presence of God was everywhere, anywhere, but where you were. But the spirit of God is an indwelling spirit. It seeks to express through you, right here and right now. Think on the words of Jesus the Christ when he exclaimed, "If I do not find one worthy, I will command the rocks to shout out my name."

We want to say, in substance, "Jesus, you don't have to do that. We're stepping up to the plate! We're going to allow our entire being to shout out the name and the nature of eternity, the name and the nature of life. We are going to celebrate all that is real and eternal within us."

Once, when Rickie and I were traveling from Florida to Arizona for an event, we missed our flight and got stuck at the airport. While we were delayed, I went into one of the airport stores to get some water. As I walked into the store, I heard our brother Carl Anderson singing over the PA system. Now, Carl Anderson had made his transition a few years before. In fact, the anniversary of his passing was the following day and the date of his birth was also coming up. So Rickie and I had been in the conversation about Carl, having a walk down memory lane and sending him love, just a few minutes before I walked into the store and heard his voice.

I said to myself, "This sounds familiar." As I listened closer, I said, "That's Carl Anderson, coming through the speakers!" I immediately asked one of the women working in the store, "Where is this coming from?" She replied, "I don't know, I think it's coming in from a satellite."

I dropped the stuff I was buying on the counter and ran back to where Rickie was sitting. I said, "Carl's on the radio, you know, and I think it's our CD from Agape." She came back inside with me and we listened to our friend Carl sing "I'm Ready to Listen Now." It was a profound and moving moment for both of us. I felt really good about it as I got back in line to pay. The next song that came on was Carl singing another of our songs, "I Am the Rock." Rickie and I and a few other people stood there listening to Carl proclaim, "I am the rock, I'm your place of salvation."

The woman I'd been speaking with asked, "You know this song?" I said, "Me and my wife wrote this song."

Rickie and I walked away wondering how Carl—singing our song—got on the radio like this. We could still hear him singing another song, "You

Anointed Me." Rickie turned to me and said, "You know, it's an interesting phenomenon that whenever you leave, I can't hear Carl, but when you're here, I can hear him." Then I reached into my pocket for my phone, and another of Carl's songs was playing on my iPhone.

The point of this story is that there's always a broadcast emanating from within us. This eternal broadcast is saying, "I am that I am. I am alive. I am life. I am all that I am." Heretofore, if someone told you that heaven was merely in the sky, they told you a lie. If they told you that good is somewhere other than where you are, they told you a lie. You're here to rebroadcast the heavenly broadcast without stepping it down one little bit.

As you step out of your own way—which means releasing your perceptions, ego, and the limited thought forms of who and what you really are—you'll begin to broadcast the great I Am presence. That energy will congeal around you and create pathways to righteousness. It will become the staircases to ever-expanding good. You will see it outpicturing as all of your needs met, ideal employment, and true friendships. The presence becomes everything that's necessary in your life, when you realize you're not separated from it.

Rickie and I heard Carl Anderson singing "I'm Ready to Listen Now." He was reminding us that, besides our outer ear, we have an inner ear that allows us to hear the inaudible, the things which can't be caught by the five senses. There's an angel of eternal progression whispering into our inner ear, telling us that that we're more than meets the eye and that there's something within that must be expressed.

When we forge into our spiritual practice—our prayer, meditation, contemplation, reflection, sacred service, study, and fellowship—with a sincerity that comes from having meaningful insight, we enable ourselves to hear beyond what the physical ear can bring us. We begin to see that we're connected by much more than what we've inherited from our parents and society and from our human experience. There's something about us that comes directly from the divine presence. When we attune our inner ear to hear the inaudible and our inner eye to see the invisible, we are able to do what the world calls impossible. We're up for the challenge and the transformation that comes with it.

Another song that we heard from Carl that day was "You Anointed Me," written by Erik Peterson. "You Anointed Me" speaks to the fact that we are anointed, and appointed, by the holy spirit. You don't have to be voted in by Congress. You don't have to be validated by the Senate. You don't have to be vetted by society. You are anointed and appointed by the spirit of the living God to do great works. You don't have to look to man, whose breath is in his nostrils, for any kind of validation. You don't have to look outside of yourself for any kind of worthiness. No! As the spiritual image and likeness of ultimate reality, you are anointed and appointed to set your life free, to discover the gifts, talents, and capacities within you that are beyond your wildest imagination. You have a mandate to put forth another face of divinity. You've been appointed by the presence to give your unique gifts, to share love, and to reveal peace and plentitude.

When Carl Anderson sang, "I am the rock. I am your place of salvation," he was saying, in substance, that we are to lean on the infinite invisible, that which is real and eternal. As we become keenly interested in the presence, we begin to see it everywhere. We gain the insight to lean into it, and allow it to support the weight of our being.

Up to this moment, you may have been leaning on your cunning, your intellectual skill, or any of the other things that you learned in this dimension. You may have been leaning on your degrees, your money in the bank, depending on the things that you can see. And that's alright. But as you look out upon the vicissitudes of the human experience, you can see that those things change all the time. You can't bank on them. You can't even bank on the bank.

The world of phenomena is in a state of constant change. People are worried and doubtful and nervous, because they're banking on banks.

They're banking on what's visible, what they can touch, what's apparent to the five senses. But spirit says, "I am the rock. I am your place of salvation. I am your all in all." When we become keenly interested in this realm, it starts to become more real to us than the very chairs we sit on. And we begin to recognize the different mind-sets that either encourage and enable this interest to grow, or those that hinder it.

Hindering mind sets, which have a tendency to block the flow, are steeped in curiosity, inquisitiveness, and scrutiny. If you're merely curious, you're a looky-loo, just wanting to see what's happening without getting involved. If you are inquisitive, you're like the paparazzi, invading other people's territory and trespassing. If you're constantly scrutinizing, you're always looking for what's wrong. These mind-sets keep you tied to a very small, myopic perception. You don't get a chance to see the way things really are, and you end up complaining and blaming, which is a public declaration of your inability to see the Christ. You end up becoming a self-fulfilling prophecy of all the negativity that you have found, because you've been looking for it.

And then there's interest. Interest is different. It comes from a root word in the Latin context that means "to love." When you're really interested in something, you fall in love with it. There's an opening. You become involved with it. You even wonder how you missed it all of this time. Of course, the object of your interest has been here all of the time, calling out to you, but, perhaps, at the time you were merely curious. You were merely inquisitive. Or you took to long scrutinizing it, looking for flaws. But when you're interested, the thing that you're interested in takes over your life.

For example, many years ago I discovered this brand-new vegetarian store and restaurant. My dietary interests had recently shifted, and I was so happy that I came upon this new place. When I went inside, I said, "Oh my God, this is beautiful. How long have you been here?" And the proprietor said, "Twenty years."

I couldn't believe it. I'd been driving down the same street for 20 years. But I never saw it before, because it wasn't in my interest. In that same sense, when you become interested in the divine realm, after a while, that's all you see. When you choose to become more yourself, you suddenly begin to hear the still, small voice all around, guiding you toward your passion and purpose. When you are interested in leaning on the realm of the ineffable, you see the face of God all around you. You live in a whole different world. God becomes more real to you than anything.

It doesn't matter if you've used defence mechanisms to keep God out in the past. It doesn't matter what coping mechanisms you have. It doesn't matter if you've engaged in compulsive behaviors. Resentment, animosity, fear, doubt, worry, skepticism, and cynicism—none of these things can keep the presence of God at bay if you've shown that you have an authentic interest in knowing Him. God has eternity to get past your defences. The presence is knocking on the door and waiting. At some point, it's going to get through. You may have a sudden insight, a sudden expanded point of view, a sudden *aha!* moment. That's the spirit of God taking over. It's beckoning you to become more yourself.

The spiritual stimulus package, as I've indicated, begins with this type of inner broadcast, an awareness that nothing about you needs to be fixed, and nothing needs to be added. We are all here to download and reveal our gifts on this planet with ease, grace, and powerful spiritual dignity. It takes strength to lean on the invisible, because the surface mind wants you to lean on your quantifiable strengths and your intellect. It wants you to lean on all the things that you've been told you can depend on. But to mature spiritually, sometimes you just have to do things that appear crazy to others. Leaning on the infinite invisible elicits a sense of joy that is like nothing else.

When you lean on the spirit, people may think you're a little odd. You may say cryptic things that don't make any sense in the linear space. But that's okay. You're coming from a much, much wider space, because your stimulus package begins with an awareness that you have a source that never runs out. Your stimulus package tells you that if you will but listen, you'll be guided. Your self-worth doesn't come from people outside of yourself. Our stimulus package includes the awareness, right here and right now, that God is our rock and our salvation.

Look at your life right now, and see if there are any areas that you're worried or concerned about. Know that the negativity that stems from worry is simply a congealed lie, which has condensed itself into an experience. But by embracing your stimulus package, by becoming interested in it, you can unravel the lies. You can be set free, your heart mended, your soul healed. The shell of cynicism and skepticism around your heart will dissolve as you joyfully stand in the truth that all of your needs are met. In spite of the rumbling discord of our culture, you can demonstrate that you're connected to the presence, and able to reveal harmonizing prosperity and ever-increasing gratitude.

Train your awareness to see that you're surrounded by beauty. Invite your consciousness to expand to embrace the fact that you're surrounded by infinite supply. Let your awareness show you that all that you desire is here. The poise, the confidence, the prosperity, the wealth, the abundance are already present. This isn't about materialism; its about harmony, health, and wholeness. See that which you most desire is consciousness, while continuously affirming to yourself that all of your needs are met. See the fulfillment of that intention in consciousness. God is for you and not against you. Everything is working together for your good.

This word is speaking itself into expression now, saying, "I am your life. I am the rock, the place of your salvation. I am your everything." In gratitude and thanksgiving, we hear that which can't be heard. We feel, see, and hear that we are connected, an emanation of the presence. We call forth divine and compelling right action in every area of our life.

The body of our affairs is designed to reveal the fundamental order of the universe, just as we're here to reveal and to reflect the cosmic order. We're not here to reflect and reveal the thoughts of our parents or our society. Nor are we here to reflect and reveal every extraneous detail of our experience. We're here to reflect the order of the cosmos, which is harmonizing good, beauty, creativity, and joy beyond our wildest imagination.

Everything that is necessary for the quantum leap into a greater expression of ultimate reality has already been provided. You have only to stand in agreement that you embrace a new beginning for your life, a new law of our life called grace.

Adventure In Paradise

Take a breath, right here
Take a holy breath, right here
I'm taking an adventure
I'm taking an adventure in paradise

As we're lifted up into the spiritual domain
We begin to see a little bit differently
There's a broadcast going on
This broadcast comes from within you
There's a song singing in you

There is something within you that
wants to express
There is something within you that
wants to come forward
You are anointed and appointed by the
Spirit as the image and likeness of Divine and ultimate reality
As we hang in that domain we bring heaven to earth as a spiritual prac-
tice, wake up and say to yourself

"I'm taking an adventure in paradise
And guess what? I'm taking you with me!
I'm activating my spiritual
stimulus package
I'm taking an adventure in paradise"
Your stimulus package begins with an awareness
That you're sourced and fueled and funded

By a renewable resource which is within you
It never runs out, it is your Essence, it's your life

Your Divine spiritual stimulus package
Is activating the gifts of Divinity within you
That you may express them
You will express them beyond your
wildest imagination
And joy, joy breaks out all over
It's the real Source
Feel it! Feel it in your bones
Take a holy breath and say to yourself

In order to have this stimulus package
Stop looking outside for help
Become still and listen, listen with that inner ear
Life is everywhere, joy is everywhere

2   Let It Be Alright

Know that you're coming from plenitude and abundance
You lack nothing! Nothing!
You have star power
You are the way the stars look back at themselves
You have star power!
With that motivation underlying every action that you take
You are to boldly go where no woman or no man
Has ever gone before

There is a vitalizing energy moving through you, a dynamic field of infinite potential rising up and seeking to become conscious of itself as you. Scripture refers to this energy as the light that lighteth up every man and woman that cometh into the world. We want to turn our full attention toward that light of God within us. So, for a moment, pull yourself away from the world of effects, circumstances, situations, anything that would hinder this awareness.

Sometimes this is easier said than done. Perhaps you've been beset by mortal-minded thinking or the opinions of others. Maybe you've been overwhelmed by what other people are thinking about what you're thinking, about what they're thinking about. Perhaps you've fallen under the aegis of the hypnotic spell of a media that would turn your attention toward that which is contentious or is glamorizing that which is superficial.

If we allow it, the world can be full of distractions that hinder us from moving in the direction of our good. But you're here to take back your power. Pull your attention to the very center of your being and come to an understanding that you have real, bona fide star power. A noted scientist once said that human beings are the star system becoming conscious of itself. Think about that for a moment. All the power of the cosmos, all the power that is producing millions and millions of galaxies at millions of miles a minute—all that power is within you, right now.

Perhaps you've been swayed by popular opinion that star power has something to do with celebrity.

We hear the term "star power" and our mind automatically goes to some tabloid reports about what Britney Spears had for lunch yesterday. But real star power is what you are. You have the power of psychogenesis. At any given point in time, you have within you everything required to begin your whole life all over again. When you remove your attention from the external world, when you pull your mind out of the sea of mental garbage, you can begin your life anew. There are incarcerated individuals who've discovered this truth. Others have come to this awareness after having been hospitalized. A person might be a refugee in exile, an inmate languishing in a self-made prison. Just look at Malcolm X, Nelson Mandela, and Geronimo Pratt, all of whom have experienced imprisonment. Mitchell May, founder of the Synergy Company, discovered this truth while languishing in a hospital bed when he was pronounced dead after a traumatic car crash. Not only did Mitchell survive, during the course of his recovery his body regenerated nerve endings and healed other injuries that doctors said were literally impossible. His Holiness the Dalai Lama discovered the way to begin again after he was exiled from Tibet. Now the entire world is his home.

These individuals were committed to shining the light of God no matter what happened to them or what circumstance they faced. The light that "lighteth up every man and every woman that cometh into the world" is not the little light that is sung about in the song "This Little Light of Mine." We're not using terms like "little," which denote quantity. We're speaking in terms of being an individual light that has the same magnitude as the stars, the same magnitude as the light and the life of God, because there's only one light, only one life, which is our individual life.

Not long ago when I was interviewed on a radio program, the host asked me to define what a cult is. Another minister who was also on the show asked me where the future of religion is headed. I defined a cult as a group of individuals that don't aspire to go beyond the consciousness of the leader of their particular group, those who don't seek to shine their own light or do their own inner work.

Cult members are content to ride on the coattails of someone else's belief or revelation regardless of where it might lead. As for the future of religion, I said, "Well, when you fast-forward, a day will come when traditional religions will seem like museum exhibits. Children will say to their parents, 'Did people really separate themselves from each other because they were Christians, Jews, Buddhists, or Muslims?'"

And we'll say, "Yes, it used to be that way until people began to have direct insight into universal spiritual laws and principles. They began to see that as this global consciousness emerged, mainstream religions were no longer necessary."

Human beings are primed to begin again, leaving behind beliefs which separate and divide humanity. I'm not blaspheming anything; it's the religions themselves that blasphemed the life of God by saying, "I'm the only one." Where there's no limitation placed on God, there is no blasphemy. As we begin to have personal insights around that realization through our prayer, meditation, contemplation, and spiritual study, we're motivated to wake up. Having a spiritual realization of our oneness with God opens us up to the revelation of the ever-expanding good—the kingdom of God on Earth as it is in the mind of God.

I'm sure the surface mind is asking, "How do we do this?" First, you want to stay away from dangerous people. And the most dangerous people on the planet right now are those without a dream, without a vision for their lives. Why are they a danger to themselves and everyone around them? Because they're operating under the aegis of the status quo. They're seeking to be anti-bored until they die. A person mired in such a limited state of mind is constantly being run by things that have already happened in the past, or by the thought forms of society. They're not stretching to become ever more of their true selves. They've forgotten that they have an inner calling, a call which has nothing to do with convenience or comfort. Rather, it's a call for us to constantly progress, evolve, and share more of the light that's within us.

So, right now, hear this warning: stay away from dangerous people! Stay away from people who are complaining all the time. Stay away from individuals who constantly see themselves as victims, because it can rub off on you; you'll discover that you're no longer reaching and expanding into who and what you really are. Instead, you will be trapped in complacency, apathy, and lethargy, no longer motivated to wake up. Staying in line with the status quo will keep you from being motivated to sacrifice the lesser for the greater, and to download the realm of ever-expanding good in your life.

Throughout the course of your day, periodically stop and ask yourself, "Where am I coming from?" Notice whether what you were about to do or say was motivated by a reactive quality, meaning the surface mind reacting to a circumstance or a cause that was already set in motion by someone else.

Or, were you coming from the field of plenitude and abundance, the field of the living intelligence that governs the universe? Are you offering a divine response to life from the midst of your soul? If, in truth, you discover that you're coming from the reactionary side of yourself, stop and begin again. Make an in-course correction.

Sometimes we come from the field of irritation, from a mind-set of taking everything personally, or "My past is so laden with negativity, I can't even see a future." Sometime we come from lack, limitation, not-enough-ness. But no matter where we come from, we can begin in this moment to come from a higher consciousness, from the dimension of our soul that has the freedom to think independently of circumstances.

Right now, you can enter into the realm of the presence of God, the presence of the inspired wisdom of the universe, and act from that dimension. You can temporarily bracket the things of the world that appear to be so big, heavy, and oppressive. It doesn't matter if you're in a jail cell, a hospital ward, or a self-made prison where you find yourself taking things personally and being constantly offended by the world. You can start over, allowing your life to spin and unfold from the eternal rather than from time.

Feel and sense that you're truly free, that you're not here merely to get rid of negativity in your life. Feel that there's an underlying motivation behind everything you do, an underlying motivation to wake up. The divine impulse within you seeks to become more aware of your intrinsic Christ nature, your Buddha nature. You can place your attention there right now and enable yourself to live from that state of inner freedom through a conscious choice to do so.

Choose to be free right now. The surface mind may be describing the prison that you're in: I don't have enough money. I don't have enough time. No one likes me. They said something about me. They didn't do it right. Your description of circumstances may feel accurate, but you don't have to remain imprisoned in it. What happens next in your life all depends on what happens next in your mind. Harboring negative thoughts coagulates them into experiences. But you can be free right now. Consciously choose this day whom you shall serve, what you shall serve, and how you shall serve. Choose. Ask yourself at any given moment, "Where am I coming from?"

Take a breath and allow yourself to become aware of the field of infinite possibilities surrounding you. See through the façade of your life, through the baggage of history, to the freedom of your infinite potential. Give yourself permission to live the true purpose of your incarnation. Feel yourself grounded in the energy of high potential. Embrace yourself in a consciousness of unconditional love. As you do this, know that you're also embracing your entire community, even the entire world.

Give yourself permission to shake off the dust of the world. Shake off impossibility thinking, because nothing is impossible with God. You have star power. The true light is the light that lighteth up every man and woman that cometh into the world. It's not about religion, it's about liberation—liberating your mind from misguided thoughts about reality so that instead you have direct contact with reality. Your star power makes you a laser beam of God-energy.

Free yourself from any mental, emotional, physical, or societal prisons in which you have boxed yourself. Free yourself from creating your next moment based on opinions of the past. Create your next moment on an in-the-beginning consciousness: In the beginning, I'm coming from God consciousness. In the beginning, I live in the now moment. In the beginning, there's plenitude in my life. In the beginning, I radiate abundance. In the beginning, I know who I am.

What spins out from such an awareness is a direct expression of infinite potentiality. The motivation underneath everything that you're doing then becomes about allowing yourself to be a beneficial presence on the planet. With this as your motivation, you create no obstacles for the fulfillment of your divine destiny. All obstacles are a projection of a belief in obstacles. Instead, open the divine circuits within you by getting the ego out of the way.

Take a deep breath, and as you do so, feel your freedom in that breath. Feel what it would be like if you had not one complaint about anything, if you took nothing personally. Feel what the vibration of your body temple would be if nothing bothered you. Feel that energy rising up inside you, becoming stronger and more powerful.

Don't allow the surface mind to have dominion over you. You're free. Establish a level of freedom in which you can feel what it would be like not to get ruffled, to live in a complaint-free environment. Allow your interior awareness to remain focused there by reminding yourself that you are the star system looking back at itself. Whenever you look up and see a beautiful star, understand that you are the evolution of that star becoming conscious of itself. If you have the same magnitude of power that's birthing galaxies at millions of miles a minute, you would be confident that you could pay your rent, that you would manifest what you need when you need it. But you're not going to accomplish these things through any form of manipulation. You're only going to do it by expanding your awareness of the presence of God.

Get your stuff together! Consciously choose the path of expanding awareness. If you have to pray, meditate, and do affirmations every single day until you convince yourself that all of your needs are met, do it! Sit there until you convince yourself that whatever "they" said is unhealable is already healed in your life. Convince yourself that the universe is for you and that nothing is against you. When you're truly convinced, the outside world will have no power over you. You will be free.

As you continue to do your work, you'll come out of the realm of victimhood and begin to establish a sacred vision for your life. You start to see the world that you want to live in and walk in that direction. In the beginning, this happens through personal volition, through willpower. You make a choice to do something, and it happens along the way. You moved from personal volition to embodying a state of being, which effortlessly attracts into your life all that is necessary for your continued growth. Instead of saying "I want this" or "I must get that," you'll live from a space that says, "I've become a conscious field of goodness. What I already have within me and around me generates everything that I need." Then you can sit back and watch as your good shows up in the most unexpected, out-of-the-way possibilities. This happens because you've activated your inner empowerment in which the miraculous will take place.

Remind yourself that it's not by might but by your spirit that you evolve. Grace is already accompanying you, blessing you, cheering you on, guiding and guarding you. Feel confident and breathe a sigh of relief, because in truth you've already arrived. You're now at the top of the mountain seeing a new horizon.

Amplify this realization with your gratitude. Let your mind go on a search for everything in your life for which you can be grateful. Just let it overwhelm you. In this field of thanksgiving, this field of high appreciation, we see more clearly. All of the mental and emotional debris that has created a spiritual cognitive
deficiency is being cleaned up right now. We see that the presence and the power and the love of God almighty, God all-beauty, is right where we are.

Let It Be Alright

Take a breath
Where you comin' from?
Let it be alright to be alright
Take a breath

When we're talking about
the topic of the God Light
We're talking star power
We're talking power of the Kosmos
And that we are here to beam
this Light of ours
To such a degree that
we're becoming aware
Of what's seeking to express itself through
you Feel your freedom right now
You are free to think in this moment
This God Light of mine, I'm gonna
let it shine!

Let it be alright to be alright
Let it be alright to be alright
Let it be alright to be alright
Let it be alright, let it be alright

You have to ask yourself on a regular basis
Where am I coming from?

This will purify your motivation

Your motivation is to, one: wake up
And two: to be a beneficial presence
on the planet
To give your gifts
With that motivation underlying every
action that you take
You are to boldly go where no woman
or no man
Has ever gone before

Know that you're coming from plenitude
and abundance
You lack nothing! Nothing!
You have star power
You are the way the stars look back
at themselves
You have star power!
With that motivation underlying every
action that you take
You are to boldly go where no woman
or no man ware
Of what's seeking to express itself
through you
Feel your freedom right now
You are free to think in this moment

3   Who Loves You, Baby

There is a presence of Love
That is seeking to express itself through you
Self-love and appreciation is the beginning step
Of allowing that which does not belong
To be uncovered, dissolved, and evaporated
In the sunlight of God's Love
And it takes back the past, rolls it up, and dissolves it
Into nothingness, and the nowness of this moment breaks free

This Love is always shining

When we allow ourselves to be drenched in the sunlight of God's love, we step into a field of possibility in which the work of creating and becoming is already done. We exude the divine love of this energetic field in magnificent, unique, and beautiful ways. As you look around at your life, take the opportunity to notice the beauty that's there. Wherever you are, know that you're part of a community of individuals who are seeking to pierce the three-dimensional veil and see the world the way it really is, beyond the "facts" of life. More and more, people are waking up to the realization that what we consider "facts" are often lies that have congealed as circumstances and situations.

The truth is that we're living, moving, and having our beingness in the great power, the presence, and the love of God. As we fine-tune our awareness, we begin the process of going beyond the sense of separation between us and our good, between us and the love that's within us. This way of being may not be in lockstep with society, because our societies often mirror whatever is popular, rather than what is real, necessary, and true. Walking a spiritual path, or being part of a spiritual community, is about being reminded, each and every day, of the love and peace and joy and harmony that's available to us at all times. We're here to remind ourselves of the sacred truth that there's way more than meets the eye within us. We're here to pierce through any sense of separation or distance, to catch a glimpse of who and what we really are.

Becoming immersed in that field of possibility enables us to birth and rebirth our transcendent self into this dimension. Eternity keeps coming forward in time, over and over and over again. If we fall into opinions or narrow paradigms and points of view, we can catch ourselves quickly so that we ultimately start living from this expanded awareness. We also come to recognize that fear, doubt, and worry are the altered states of consciousness, and that love, joy, awe, wonder, and peace are our natural state of being.

We're here to remind ourselves to come out of the altered state and to step into our authentic state, which is God consciousness. The spirit of

God is saying, in essence, "I got you! I got you in my heart! I got you in prayer! I know the truth about you! I'm holding that space for you! You can lean on this field! All is well!"

I remember once taking a trip to the Transformation Leadership Conference in Bermuda. I'd just left my wife, Rickie BB, after having completed a workshop in Omega the week before. While she was still at the conference, she sent me an e-mail. Her words were a beautiful love letter and, as I read it, it knocked me out inside. This expression of love caused me to stop and reflect. My reflection then bounced from the note to other individuals in my life. I became keenly aware of their love for me, my love for them, my love for God. I just love.

That awareness morphed into a recognition of how much God loves me. I tend to think about how much I love God and how I've surrendered my life to the presence. But this particular insight allowed me to catch just how much I'm embraced and loved by the holy presence in return. In the instant of that reflection, my consciousness expanded and I felt myself more receptive, more available, more open to the love, peace, harmony, and abundance that is all around us. The energy began to flow through me in an unprecedented way when I caught a deeper understanding of just how much God loves me.

Stop and ask yourself the question, "Who loves you, baby?" Then take a moment to reflect on just how much we are really loved, supported, and taken care of. Become aware of how many people are holding you in a space of love. A very important part of the spiritual work that we do involves removing the filters from our own awareness, so as not to project our beliefs, opinions, and judgments onto others. We want to see the truth about other individuals and live from the state of uplifted consciousness, which allows that intention to manifest. At the same time, however, we have to reflect on our own worth and open ourselves up to see just how much we're appreciated and loved by the universal presence.

When you're around someone who loves you unconditionally, you become aware that they have no judgment about you. You become aware that they've suspended their beliefs and opinions about anything that may have happened in your life. There are no projections going on. Your loved ones are able to see through your foibles or personality quirks, straight to the essence of your being. No matter what happens in the outside world, those that love you are able to hold the space of support, acceptance, and encouragement, seeing you at your best and highest, regardless of the situation.

On a regular basis, we must take time out to reflect on ourselves beyond narrow opinions, perceptions, and projections from the world. We must release the judgments that we sometimes carry about ourselves about things that aren't complete within us or things that remains to be done before we can be "okay." There are all kinds of ways that we hold ourselves in abeyance from this tidal wave of love that's rushing toward us. But if we could take time out on a regular basis and feel into the perfection of the spirit of God that adores us just as we are, we'd begin the process of allowing that love to rush over us and transform our entire existence.

Give yourself permission to forgive your mistakes and misperceptions. Let yourself off the hook for times that you may have misspoken, allowing things to fly out of your mouth that you wish you could reel back in. On a regular basis, every single day, take time out and begin to see yourself without all of the gunk of your own personal judgments. Ease into the awareness that there's a presence of love seeking to express itself through you. But it can only come through the openness that you provide through your sense of self-love and appreciation.

Keep in mind, we're not talking about self-love from an ego sense, but from a sense of stopping the mental chatter about what's wrong or what's not complete within you. Self-love is about releasing the voices of judgment, which are quick to remind you of all the things you have to do before you can have perfection in your life. The spirit of self-love is the still, small voice within you, encouraging you to come to a complete stop on a regular basis and breathe into the awareness of how deeply you're loved.

You can start doing that by finding one or two people who you know have your back, regardless of what's going on in your life. These people love you and appreciate you just as you are. Now, begin to drill deep into the awareness of how they see you. As you do this, suspend your opinion about yourself, what you believe is worthwhile and what's incomplete. Just bask in the feeling of being loved. Then, using that feeling as a springboard, open yourself to the love of the spirit. Feel how it holds you and appreciates you and supports you. Then, if you allow yourself to hang there for a little while, you'll feel your heart burst open to a flood of unconditional love.

This love has nothing to do with accomplishment. It has nothing to do with a merit or demerit system. It is simply the love of God rushing to express itself through you. From this space of openness and awareness, you can begin to see that self-love and appreciation is not an endgame. It's a beginning for your growth, development, and unfoldment. It's where you take the first baby steps of transformation, which makes the journey so much smoother.

Rather than trying to fix everything that you believe is wrong with yourself, all the foibles and shortcomings, step into this vibration of self-love and appreciation. It allows that which does not belong to you to be uncovered, dissolved, and evaporated in the sunlight of God's love. This ineffable, dynamic presence is like the rays of the sun that are always glowing, regardless of clouds of doubt, worry, fear, and separation. This love is always shining.

When you do this, you've made yourself receptive to the very miracles you want to happen in your life. You've made yourself receptive to the grace of God that is seeking to happen in your life. Grace can't be earned. It can't be made. But you can make it welcome. You can become the condition for grace and love to take over every circumstance and situation of your life. But to do that means stopping the mental chatter that would seek to hinder your growth.

Letting go of the mental chatter requires standing at the mid-place, where we're not falling into a heavy ego trip about how wonderful we are, but at the same time not going into heavy denigration about what's wrong or bad. Standing in the mid-place of being and becoming means appreciating all that you are, while knowing that you're barely scratching the surface of that which is trying to emerge. It's a beautiful process that's well-oiled with the unconditional love and receptivity of the spirit.

It incites a quickening in your heart, a quickening in your being, and you begin to walk in the awareness that you're divinely supported, maintained, and sustained by all of life. You begin to walk in the awareness that we do, in fact, live in a friendly universe. You believe that, truly, everything is working together for your good. You maintain the awareness that God is for you and that there's nothing against you. You pop out of the cause-and-effect relationships that predominate in a Newtonian worldview, and you begin to see that you're a part of a quantum reality, in which there's no cause and effect anywhere. There's only this one presence emerging and being itself everywhere. From that space, all that exists is potentialities of the essence of God trying to express itself, waiting for the right condition to do so. Nothing external causes anything to happen, because everything has already happened in the mind of God. All of creation exists as a seed idea, waiting for the proper condition to enable it to emerge as your life.

Your self-love and appreciation, which encompass a willingness to embrace and be receptive to the good that's all around you, become the right condition for that which has already happened in the mind of God to ooze into expression as you. It takes back the past, rolls it up, and dissolves it into nothingness. The nowness of this moment breaks free as you. In the process, your needs are met. The healing happens. The body temple responds. The mental body becomes clarified. The emotional body becomes purified. The body of your affairs begins to reflect and reveal the cosmic order of the universal presence. This presence is everywhere in its fullness, waiting for the right condition to show up and say, "Surprise! It's me! Who loves you, baby? Who loves you? Who's got your back? Who's made you in Its own image and lightness? Who's given you everything? You're missing nothing! Who's poured Its entire being into you? Who loves you, baby?"

This is what the spirit of the living God is saying. So stop trying to fix yourself. Instead, on a regular basis, start seeing yourself as the image and likeness of spirit, the divine and perfect expression of this eternal presence. Then watch as the negative thoughts that have been anchored in your mind for so long, trapped in a sea of mental garbage, dissipate. You'll have the opportunity to disconnect yourself from the limiting perceptions of a world that only sees in parts, that takes snapshots and makes whole stories out of it. You'll recognize yourself as a singular manifestation of a cosmic destiny that is unfolding forever. But you need the fuel of self-love and appreciation to allow this divine engine to purr, to grow and unfold, becoming ever more itself.

Who loves you, baby? You are loved by Love itself.

The presence of the living God loves to live through you as a healthy, prosperous, creative, generous being. Why? Because the conditions for unhindered expression exist in such beings. It's not that God doesn't love every single aspect of its creation, but it loves the places that it gets to play freely and express its full potential. As Emanuel Swedenborg said, "God suffers a stillbirth into humanity until we act by the good that we already know." God suffers a stillbirth until we choose to fall in love with what's here, until we say yes to life, until we can see beyond the dimness of eternity and recognize that there's only the power of the presence of the love of God everywhere. The presence of God is waiting patiently for that opening.

You are that opening.

Who loves you, baby? It's the presence of God. Take a moment to return in your mind to your thoughts about the people in your life who love you unconditionally. You can be in a crazy mood or be feeling divine; they don't care. These people have got your back. Breathe in and hold the space of that love. Feel how much they love you. Exhale, and then take another breath, just a little bit deeper, as you amplify that field of love in your awareness. Allow yourself to luxuriate in how much you're loved and appreciated. Notice that, as you're immersed in this feeling, you're suspending any beliefs about what's supposedly wrong with you. You're suspending any beliefs that there's something within you that has to be fixed or improved. You're suspending, for a moment, any projections that have been placed upon you by the world.

Now breathe into the awareness of how much you love the presence of God (not the anthropomorphic representation of God, but this presence that is Love itself and is conscious of itself everywhere). Reflect now on how this presence of love is always giving. It has no withhold button in it. It doesn't take a time-out from giving of itself—ever. It doesn't run out of love or energy. It doesn't run out of ideas. It's always expressing the unconditional love that is the essence of it's nature.

I'll always remember a number of years ago when I had a spiritual opening, and I could see just how beautiful this presence was and how it loved me as if I was the only being in existence. It loves everyone the same way. Feel into this deep love, the love of God for you, the love of your friendships, your soulships, your beloveds around you. And continue to breathe into the awareness that you're alright exactly the way you are. You may have stumbled and fell, but you're alright. You may not think you have everything you need in this world, but you're alright. You may not have accomplished what you think you should have accomplished by this time, but you're alright. There may be some incomplete things in your human existence that you want to get together, but you're alright.

This sense of alrightness becomes a part of the condition that allows for the brilliant ideas within you to take root and express themselves. The spirit of God responds by corresponding to its own nature in you. And when you can rise up to this level of self-love and appreciation, the condition for God to express a new idea or insight is ripe. It expresses as an open door. It expresses as a divine answer. It expresses as wisdom, guidance, and direction. It expresses in a language, and in a way, that you can understand.

This is the original blessing that God has bestowed on every one of us. But we must be willing to receive this blessing, to accept and activate it. We must say yes to it. Through the energy of our yes, our lives begin to requalify. The thought forms that have out-pictured themselves as lack, limitation, fear, doubt, worry, disease, disharmony, and discontent are transmuted into a wide-open field of infinite possibilities.

Step into this field of possibility. Through the lens of self-love and appreciation, see all of your needs met. Feel dynamic health coursing through the body temple right now. Feel that no hurt, harm, or danger can come nigh your dwelling place, because you're making the most high God your habitation.

As you walk on the earth and you see a flower, it's saying to you, "Who loves you, baby?" As you see the trees gently swaying in your backyard, they're saying, "Who loves you, baby?" As you see the beauty of the world around you, let it seep into your heart and hear the voice of God saying, "I love you. Accept this love. Open up. Open up your heart. Open up your heart. Accept it. Accept it."

In *The Science of Mind,* Earnest Holmes wrote, "Never was there a cosmic famine. We may stumble, but always there is that Eternal Voice, forever whispering within our ear, that thing which causes the eternal quest, that thing which forever sings and sings."

This thing, this presence, is forever singing within us, loving us, and waiting for an opening. That opening is that self-love and appreciation. In that high vibration, we can open ourselves to receive everything that the presence is giving. Remember, the presence doesn't withhold blessings. You don't pray to change the mind of God or to talk him into giving you something. You pray to come into a receptive space, in which you are available to the truth that the presence is always giving and being.

Who loves you, baby? The spirit of the living God.

Affirmation

I am loved and appreciated by the infinite presence
of God almighty. The conditions within me correspond to
God's loving and insights break free. Miracles happen.
All of my needs are met. I may not be able to see it physically.
But I'm living it now. All of my needs are met.
I am deeply loved and appreciated. And I feel it in my bones.

Who Loves You, Baby

This Love is always shining
Invite the awareness of how deeply you are loved
You can begin to do that by just finding one or two
people in your life that you know
Regardless of what's going on in your life
They got your back
Like the rays of the sun regardless of clouds of doubt
This Love is always shining
And then as you use that as a springboard
You begin to ask yourself
Who made you in its only image and likeness
Who's given every quality and named it You
In a unique way of configuration
Stop trying to fix yourself, start to see yourself

Who loves ya', Baby? Who's got your back?
Who loves ya'? Who loves ya'? Who loves ya' Baby, Baby?
Who loves ya', Baby? Who's got your back?
Who loves ya'? Who loves ya'? Who loves ya' Baby, Baby?

There is a presence of Love
That is seeking to express itself through you
Self-love and appreciation is the beginning step
Of allowing that which does not belong

To be uncovered, dissolved, and evaporated
In the sunlight of God's love
And it takes back the past, rolls it up, and dissolves it

Into nothingness and the nowness of this moment
breaks free

(This Love is always shining)
Take a breath here
Every single day take time out
And just begin to see yourself

(This Love is always shining)
There is a presence of Love
That is seeking to express itself through you
But it can only come through the openness that you're providing it

(This Love is always shining)
From stopping the mental chatter about what's wrong
From stopping the mental chatter about what's not complete
(This Love is always shining)

It has nothing to do with accomplishment
Nothing to do with a merit or demerit system
It is simply the love of God rushing to that place called You
(This Love is always shining)

And if you allow yourself to hang there for a little while
You begin to walk in the awareness

4   U R The Answer

Do you want to be whole?
Do you want a healing?
Do you want to live fully?
Take a breath
U R the answer
Something wonderful is always on the verge of happening
Something magnificent is always on the verge of happening
Opportunity is everywhere
It's knocking, it's knocking, it's knocking on your heart

When we rest in the Lord, we're resting in the law of life, the tremendous evolutionary impulse that governs all creation. You are here in this moment to be reminded and inspired to wake up to this reality, which lies beyond what your senses can provide. That which is eternal must first be realized in consciousness and then transmuted into form, allowing your life to become the living evidence of that which we call the power and the presence and the love of God.

When considering inspiration, focus, and resolve, we must come into an awareness that we are to expand our understanding of their impact in our lives. Inspiration is the breath of God breathing through us, pouring forth ideas that are infinite in nature. Spiritual qualities including beauty, love, joy, compassion, kindness, and creativity are universal ideas held in the mind of God. When we're inspired, these ideas flow through us naturally, looking for the right condition to express through us. By making a choice to stay in the frequency of inspiration—as you do when you when you serve, when you give, when you read an inspiring book, when you listen to uplifting music—you find yourself living from this realm, rather than reaching for it. Before you know it, there are ideas proliferating in the ideaosphere that are looking for you!

At some point, freeing the slaves in this country was just an idea in someone's mind. At some point, the elimination of the caste system in Sri Lanka was an idea. Liberation and freedom are embedded in the hearts and souls of individuals. Set loose, these ideas touched the lives of millions of more individuals, and still they continue to unfold and touch more and more people the world over. Through these ideas, ambassadors of peace, love, and goodwill take action on our planet, and we begin to see the world in its highest potentiality, as it could be—not only free of slavery and injustice, but of poverty, lack, limitation, and violence.

We want to begin to see the world as God sees it: a playground full of ideas where we can express ourselves in joy and bring about great works of art, all in the name of the expression of our souls. Perhaps then we'd eliminate the limited theism and dogmas that would have us believe that we're fallen people and instead arrive at the understanding that we are emergent people, that we're rising up to reveal more and more of God's glorious nature.

We are here to have this kind of deep understanding and to live it completely. In the ideaosphere, we're captured by the awareness that the presence of God is our very life and being. We see that something wonderful and magnificent is always on the verge of happening. Our task becomes to develop a high level of intuitive receptivity, shaking off notions of reality that are not aligned with this truth.

As we walk through the world in this way, a holy resolve builds up within us. We become on purpose about our purpose, and that purpose is to reveal the nature of God. Every human being has the purpose of waking up to this reality. Each person's vision for the expression of that purpose might be different. But when we understand our purpose and we're able to articulate a vision for fulfilling it, our lives take on the enhanced focus needed to see the vision through to its manifestation. We know why we wake up every single day. Even though there may be challenges and difficulties, we have the strength to make it through. Even though there may be delays and disappointments, we know they're not denials and never give up on ourselves.

In the Agape community, we've been encouraging something called tell-a-vision parties, where members go to each others' houses and spend the evening sharing their sacred visions about the possibilities for their lives, their neighborhoods, the nation, and the world. People come together to support each other through prayer, visioning, and fellowship. Articulating our vision supports our resolve to move forward, even when there appears to be a lack of energy, a mood like depression, simple laziness, or other obstacles. Rather than allowing a halt to our progress, the vision becomes the guiding force that reinvigorates our resolve.

The first step in this process is to come into the awareness that every single day of your life you can make a U-turn toward the universal in you, the unadulterated within you, the unified within you, the presence of God within you. You are the answer. Make a U-turn toward accepting the truths that encourages the evolution of your soul. When there is real understanding, you begin to live in the world as if open doors are everywhere. There are no closed doors, just infinite opportunities.

I sometimes think about King Solomon's fateful day when he went through a fit of soul-sickness. He had accomplished everything a man of his times could accomplish, accumulating every material thing that the world had to offer—money, power, and fame. He had all of the things he thought he needed to be happy until the soul-sickness of emptiness took him over. In that moment, he had an insight, a revelation that opened him up to becoming a man of wisdom. Solomon's introspection upon his life, accompanied by looking out upon the larger world, announced, "Vanity. Vanity. All is vanity. Striving after the wind. With all thy getting, get understanding."

His discovery brought about an inner understanding that he was here to reflect and reveal the face of God. Solomon showed true wisdom when he said, "With all of thy getting, get understanding." We're like Solomon: Sometimes we have to get to our wit's end, when things are at their toughest, before we finally come to an understanding that what we really want is the dynamic peace of mind that passes human understanding. That peace only comes from being clear about why we're here and living according to that purpose. From that perspective, you're able to live your life full-out without attachment to a desired outcome, relying instead on your full-out, unconditional commitment to living in and for the presence of God.

Phase two of understanding is to recognize that there's a spiritual faculty of intuition within you. Intuition directly accesses knowledge about something without the process of reasoning. You're here to activate that faculty so that you're not living merely from habit and guesswork, but from genuine insight. In other words, there are people who have a lot of information, knowledge stored away in their memory bank. But you are not here to be a collector of information; you're here to be an activator of the intuitive process within you.

Intuition and wisdom are within you as expressions of the living intelligence that governs the universe. When you understand something, you don't have to memorize it. In fact, when you memorize things, you don't understand them. So rather than endeavoring to live from a Memorex mind-set, recognize that you're here to experience a life of deep insight and revelation. Throw yourself open and say, "I am here to activate the gifts, the wisdom, and the intuition that is within me!" Suddenly, out of the blue, you will be blessed with an idea, an inspiration without reasoning your way through.

This is what Glenn Clark was talking about in his insightful book, *The Man Who Tapped the Secrets of the Universe*. Our goal isn't to just remember all of the world's information and be the Jeopardy winners of life. No! We want to tap into intuitive knowledge, the living intelligence that is within us. Memory may fade, and we may forget certain facts or things that have gone on in the past. But through deepening our spiritual practices of prayer, meditation, visioning, contemplation, and introspection, we can eventually find that we can recall anything we need to know when we need to know it, because omniscience is within us. That's why U R the answer.

This is the deeper level of spiritual practice: with all thy getting, get an understanding of thy purpose, thy vision. Begin to see the world the way God sees it and realize that, at a deeper level, everything you can want, hope for, or desire is already within you. Oftentimes, you'll get intuitive guidance on a need-to-know basis. That's the beautiful thing about spontaneous goodness. You don't need to stockpile it. You're not a computer. There's a part of your mind that's computer-like, and computer technology is replicating that part of the human mind. The good news is that we aren't the mind. We are avenues of pure awareness. All knowledge and wisdom is within us and we are here to set it free. Considering these truths, we can see why meditation is so pivotal, why maintaining a prayerful life is key. When we're anchored in spiritual discipline, we are less likely to be yanked around by the world of effects, circumstances, and situations. Instead, what pulls us is the supreme purpose of our life that's yearning to express itself through us. Revelations, insights, and growth cause you to live in *aha!* moments. There's no stagnation in your heart and soul, but an ever-increasing awareness that you are a spiritual idea that is forever unfolding in consciousness.

With all thy getting, get understanding that you are one with the undifferentiated, unified Presence. If you are to live this life not being pulled or cajoled by the mesmerism of world, then you have to begin to understand that we're living, moving, and having our being in something that's never divided against itself, doesn't compromise its own nature, and doesn't contradict itself. The difficulty is that we see dualistically. We compartmentalize. Viewing life from the limitations of the physical, there-dimensional realm distorts the expansiveness of the whole picture. Our senses are poor in this sense; they see through a limited lens. Nevertheless, our intuitive faculty perceives the true nature of reality. We can catch a vision of it.

To see the whole picture, you have to go into the spiritual realm and see what God forged when God thought you into existence. Everything else is sensory perception, which is a limited point of view. Making decisions based on limited perceptions creates limited results, but when we make intuitionally based decisions, they result in the evolution of the human soul and the greater collective consciousness.

You are here to tap into this undifferentiated wholeness, this sense of ultimate well-being. Granted, it's difficult to do so. Here is a story that I remembered this morning and which illustrates this point. A young boy was picking strawberries in a large field that was tangled with weeds and other kinds of berries. A man came up and said, "Son, how are you doing this? There's all kinds of weeds and berries, but you seem to just get the strawberries every time." "Sir," the boy responded, "all I see are the strawberries." His focus and resolve was to see and pick only the strawberries, and so he succeeded in his intention.

We want to move to the place where all we know is God. All we see is love. All we see are opportunities. All we see are possibilities. All we see are solutions, answers, ideas. Don't believe the aphorism that opportunity only knocks once. That's the kind of teaching that we were brought up with that is a nonsensical point of view. Opportunity ceaselessly knocks at the door of our awareness, saying, " I know you're in there! Don't try to hide. I know that good is within you. I know that love is within you. I know that peace is within you. I'm going to keep on knocking until you get tired of being knocked upon and surrender to the inner greatness I've come to reveal to you." When we begin to understand our vision and purpose, we simultaneously cultivate the ability to see the possibilities, answers, solutions, and inspirations that fulfill that vision and purpose. That's why U R the answer.

Most individuals live from a relative point of view. They make choices and decisions based on society's popular trends, which are fickle and change from moment to moment. But the universal presence and its principles are forever the same, just as gravity is always gravity. Even if you're dealing with the laws of aerodynamics or buoyancy, you still have to factor in the law of gravity, because it's always present. Practicing these universal spiritual principles on a regular basis helps us to see that our destiny is in our hands. We are taught that it's in our DNA, that it's in our cultural conditioning, or that our karma determined our destiny, but now we see through these limited points of view. Karma simply means that we shall reap what we sow, the energy we circulates returns to us, but this doesn't determine our destiny. When we make a major change in our life, whether it's a shift of focus or a shift of resolve, when we begin to unfold and become more of our true self, then the karmic propensities dissolve because they're not permanent. The only thing that is permanent is the imprimatur of God upon your own soul, the I AM immortal presence within you.

Our character determines our destiny. The right use of spiritual laws allows us to build character, to allow our authentic individuality to shine through. We don't have to rebel against authority, because a genuine iconoclast doesn't define himself by being against something; he has simply to speak the truth to individuals holding positions of authority. Individuals not in touch with their authentic uniqueness try too hard to stand out and end up covering up their brilliance with stuff that doesn't make any sense. In contrast, when we tap into the wellspring of who and what we are on the soul level, our uniqueness flowers. Our greatness shines forth and we live full-on, focused in the resolve to reveal and to manifest the glory of the living God within us.

So make that U-turn toward the undifferentiated wholeness within you. Turn toward that which is eternal on a regular basis until it sings and dances through you, until it becomes your very life and infuses your every expression. Practice the universal spiritual principles which will set you free and the world will no longer determine your fate. You'll then be able to expand during times of contraction. You'll be able to remain healthy during times of illness. You'll be able to remain in peace even though the fearful is caught in the grip of war, economic hardship, and injustice. You will walk boldly into an arena of good that brings forth the realm of heaven on earth in all that you are called to do.

Beyond a shadow of a doubt, know that it's the spirit within you that governs your life, that its love and joy within you that governs your life. Everything else is transitory, temporary, false. It has a shelf life, so why not bring eternity into time? Why not wake up, realize your eternal being now, and take that portable understanding with you everywhere you go? Why not release the faulty thoughts that you're a castoff, undeserving of heaven without being saved from original sin. No! Salvation is self-elevation through the use and living of universal spiritual principles. You don't have to wait to be happy. You can start right where you are, with what you have, with the gifts, talents, and skills you have cultivated in this very moment. Dedicate your life to the unfolding of the good that's within you, and then watch how the universe keeps giving you more materials to paint on the canvas of your life. Start now to step into your greatness, into your wholeness. God can only do for you what God can do through you. As you set yourself free, you become the triumphant victor that you are.

U Are The Answer

Do you wanna be whole?
Do you want a healing?
Do you wanna live fully?
Take a breath
U R the answer
Something wonderful is always
on the verge of happening
Something magnificent is always
on the verge of happening
Opportunity is everywhere
It's knockin', it's knockin',
it's knockin' on your heart
Set me free, let me love
Oh, opportunity is always knocking
It's knockin', it's knockin',
it's knockin' on your heart
It's knockin', it's knockin',
it's knockin' on your heart
We are surrounded by these universal
ideas of Beauty and of Love
Some of them have your name on them

U, U, YOU are the answer!
Get some understanding today
Make that U-turn
Universal, Undivided, Undeniable!

U, U, YOU are the answer!

The answer is You! It's in You!

And then there is this thing called focus
This willingness and ability to stay the course
To be so focused on that which is Real
To be so focused on that which is Eternal

We make a U-turn towards unadulterated, unified
The moment that transformation occurs
You're setting yourself free!
When you make the U-turn to the Universal Presence
And apply the Universal practices and principles
Your life is changed in a twinkling of an eye

5　One Day In Heaven

Happiness does not come from circumstances
Being the way that you want them to be
The world of phenomena does not have your happiness,
Your joy, nor your peace
That comes from Heaven
And Heaven is not a place, it is a state of consciousness
And if you really want to change the world
Wake up!

Feel your way into your connection with the spirit of the living God. Open your heart to experience a holy realization of your oneness with the power and the presence and the love of God. Bask in the awareness that pure spirit is the only life that there is, and that we're a dimension of its activity, its creativity. In turn, we bestow that energy back upon the presence as we move through this world as harbingers of its divine light. It is us, and we are a reflection of it—an image of the divine substance of the only reality that exists.

There's a mandate on our lives to be a living demonstration of that which has never been born and will never die, and to demonstrate the spiritual truth that all of our needs are always being met, if we would but turn our attention toward the activity of God rather than the disfunction of the world. Self-love is the platform, the starting point, for our pure expression throughout eternity.

This is how we begin to create heaven, which is a state of consciousness, right where we are. Sometimes, people have trouble giving up the concept that heaven is some far-off place that you go to when you die. It's not! When we speak of ever-expanding good, when we speak of the realm of continual progress, we're speaking of heaven. The over-soul, the Christ of us, is always unfolding its infinite nature. Our individual souls are particularized expressions of the over-soul, and are continuously evolving to reveal more of the greatness that's here in the moment. When we embrace a way of living in which we recognize that heaven is the realm of continual progress, we also discover that happiness, joy, and peace are a dimension of that way of life.

In other words, happiness doesn't come from external circumstances being the way you want them to be. It doesn't come when you have all of your ducks in a row, which will never happen anyway. Ever seen ducks? They don't cooperate like that. No, real happiness and peace and joy come from that embracing of continual progress of your soul.

As you're growing, as you're becoming ever more yourself, you become conscious that the world of phenomena doesn't have your happiness or your peace. Therefore, whatever happens in the world cannot take these things away from you. True happiness can only come from heaven, the consciousness of continual progress of you becoming more you—more authentic, more alive, and more awake. The world is literally transformed as individuals wake up.

Dr. Howard Thurman reminded us that if you really want to change the world, wake up! The more that people understand that the presence of God is where they are, the more the world also changes according to the awakened capacities of those individuals. That's heaven—a day in ever-expanding good and continual progress.

There are spiritual practices that allow us to stay in this progressive dimension of consciousness. These particular practices allow us to live from a heaven-on-earth perspective. A first step toward incorporating these practices is to commit to yourself that, for just one day, you'll notice and release your acquisitive nature. The acquisitive nature is the part of you that's always trying to get something external from somebody else. It believes that it needs to have something more to be happy. We all want to whet our acquisitive appetite from time to time.

There are some people who study metaphysical principles so they can whet their acquisitive appetite. They want to get more stuff to make them happy. I want you, for just one day, to just release the acquisitive nature of your being: notice it, and then drop it. If you're an entrepreneur or a businessperson, for one day choose to no longer see the people coming into your business as your customers. Stop seeing them as your bottom line, anticipating how much money you'll make from them. Instead, shift your awareness and ask the question, "How can I bring value to these individuals that are coming into my life?"

Ask yourself, "How can I give? How can I serve? How can I release more life energy?" You'll discover that you're beginning to step into the realm of progress, the realm of ever-expanding good. Now this, for some, may be a little difficult. You may find yourself having to develop your own twelve-step program. You may have to stand up and say, "I'm running amuck by getting things. I want to get stuff. I want it all! I can't pass by a mall without stopping. I'm happy when I'm buying stuff. I'm happy when I keep getting more and more stuff. At the mere thought of having one day without appeasing my acquisitive appetite, I break out in a cold sweat!"

Don't judge that particular element in your life. Simply notice it. Tell the truth about it. And then come back to the spiritual principle that you're not here to get—you're here to let. You're here to allow. You initiate that process by standing in the awareness that you already have everything you could want, hope for, or desire within your consciousness, and that you're becoming the condition through which that good is being dispensed. So you flip the script by remembering that you're here to dispense divine gifts, not to get anything. Otherwise, being focused on acquiring things that you don't really need will prevent you from being in heaven. It prevents you from progressing.

If you want to enter into heaven, just take one day of releasing your opinions. You'll discover that when you're in conversations with people, whenever somebody tries to encroach upon your opinion, when they don't agree with you, resistance flares up. Oftentimes, this is an indication that your opinions are blocking new information or insight or a new revelation. They prevent dialogue that might help you to grow and develop, or discover something you don't know right now. But your opinion, being your congealed point of view stuck on repeat, will prevent you from progressing, because whatever it is you think you know is barely the tip of the iceberg of what can be known.

For just one day, cherish no opinions. Buddhism teaches practitioners to bracket their opinions—that is, to put them aside for a moment. Acknowledge that you have an opinion and then put it aside so that you can see life freshly, without old thoughts and beliefs getting in the way of new information. Maintaining rigid positions gives you a spiritual stiff neck; you can't see the full spectrum of the power and the presence of God that is everywhere.

For one day, just one day to be in heaven, give up complaining. That's a tough one for some people. But try it. Don't engage in any complaining whatsoever. Don't belittle anyone. No talking behind anyone's back. Sometimes people can be like mental vegomatics. They slice and dice other people up all the time. Something will happen, and the mental vegomatic starts whirling away. Suddenly you're slicing and dicing the whole situation with your judgment. This isn't right! They're not right! Did you see the shoes that person had on? Oh my God!

We engage in this kind of behavior because our minds have been programmed to do so based on a fear of being out of control. The ego operates for your survival. So you complain, thinking it's going to change something. But it's not going to change anything. It just perpetuates your myopic point of view and your cognitive deficiency—your inability to see the presence of Christ everywhere that you are.

For just one day, you're going to resist the urge to blame anybody for anything. Rest assured, something will happen that your ego will insist is someone else's fault. They did that. They did it on purpose. The ego sneaks in there, and it gives you kind of a pseudo-sense of happiness, once you find the culprit for what has gone wrong in your day. It doesn't change what happened, but at least now you know who to blame! Perhaps you work in a corporate setting, where it's part of the culture of the company to assess blame when things go wrong. This is a very common scenario. And once the scapegoat is found, then business as usual can continue. Something went wrong, but as long as everyone knows that it was so-and-so's fault, people can feel (falsely) confident that the same mistakes will not be made in the future.

The impulse to blame others for our misfortunes has been around as long as people have. Back in the day, people used to blame the devil when bad things happened. Then they went to college and got a little bit sophisticated. Now they just blame their parents. That's a certain kind of evolution of consciousness. But it won't take you very far. Practice the art of not assigning blame at all, and become aware of how that one action will open your mind and your compassionate heart to move beyond any limiting beliefs.

For just one day, set an intention to develop a nonreactive attitude to phenomena of apparent negativity. Whenever something that appears to be negative is going on, choose to respond from the infinite. If you hear others complaining or casting blame, ask yourself the question, "What is my job here?" A job will show up for you because, like Jesus, you're about your father's business. You are about the business of expressing the fundamental order of the universe. And the universe is about being on display for the beauty, the love, the wholeness, and the well-being that shows up everywhere as the presence of God. What your job is not going to be is to complain, blame, or resist.

When you ask the question, "What's my job here?" you become a candidate for guidance that will speak to you in a language and a way that you can understand and act upon. You'll be guided to be a beneficial presence, an answer, an energetic vibration that corresponds with harmony and love. You will become a focal point for clarity, rather than a part of the static that perpetuates the sense of a separation from our good, putting it somewhere in the future.

Being immersed in acquisition, opinions, complaints, blame, and reaction to circumstances is like having static on the line that blocks your clear communication with spirit. Now, the word of God is always being broadcast. God doesn't turn itself on and off. God is always God. As *The Science of Mind* textbook states, "Never was there a cosmic famine. God is always God. We may stumble but always there is that eternal voice forever whispering within our ear, that thing which causes the eternal quest, that thing which forever sings and sings."

The word of God, this broadcast of beauty, love, potency, abundance, and elegant symmetry—all that's revealed in the fundamental order of existence—is always being itself everywhere. What prevents us from hearing the word of God is the static on our end of the line. Sometimes we hear it intermittently. The messages come and go, and we mistakenly think that God is coming and going, that we had a visitation from God and then we didn't.

"Where did God go?" we ask. God didn't go anywhere. Our intermittent hearing has nothing to do with the presence of God, which is the same yesterday, today, and forever. It has to do with our ability to hear and rightly see. That cannot happen if there's static on the line.

So your prayer work, your lowly listening, your meditation, and the other aspects of your spiritual practice are about eliminating the static so that you can hear properly. It's about being moved and compelled into divine right action to reveal the realm of ever-expanding good. You'll begin to notice throughout the course of the day, as you're releasing those false ideas and beliefs that we've discussed, that a degree of happiness will creep in on you. You'll find yourself looking around and trying to figure out why you're happy.

You may find yourself saying things like, "Hmm. I didn't get that phone call I was expecting. I didn't get that raise. But I found a deeper love. I'm looking around trying to figure out why this little smile is creeping on my face. Everything around me seems to be the same, but I'm happy. Where is that coming from?" You're tapping into the fundamental order of existence. The static on your life line has been mitigated, dissolved temporarily, and now you're in joy for no reason.

Circumstances will bend around that octave, that amplitude of thought and feeling. Your life changes, not because you're forcing it or trying to make it happen, but because you've gotten out of the way. In the words of Ralph Waldo Emerson, you're getting your bloated nothingness out of the way of the divine circuits and letting them flow. This is what it's about.

Allow yourself to embrace the evolutionary impulse that governs the universe. Let your soul evolve, and allow your oversoul to unfold, as you enter into the realm of progress.

From this place, you can decree a thing and watch it manifest, because you're in tune with the fundamental harmony of existence. You're not at odds with it. You're not selfish. You're not believing in a personal good that must be gained at the expense of others. There's no personal, private good where something is good for you and not good for everyone else. If it's good for you, if it's real, God good, it's good for everyone.

You can call forth your abundance and see it appear. You can call forth health and healing, right action, guidance, well-being, and creativity, because it's not about you. Your acquisitive nature isn't trying to get something or show others how you're better than they are. You're not struggling to fulfill needs that stem from a belief in lack and limitation. You've bounced out of that, and now you're finding yourself in heaven. Paradise.

Unfortunately, unchecked thoughts can ruin a good day in paradise. You wake up to a world brimming with infinite opportunities, and you can't even get out the front door without worrying. That behavior is messing up paradise. Competition also messes up paradise. Slicing and dicing people will mess up paradise. Put the mental vegomatic away before you try to walk into heaven.

Remember to ask, "How can I bring value?" No matter what you do, be aware of the value that you're bringing to others. If you engage in business, remind yourself that the only reason for any business is to bring legitimate goods and services to people, creating the condition for happiness and self-realization. That's what business and industry are all about at the highest level. Contrary to what most people believe, it's not about getting anything. It's about creating and sharing value.

This is what a day in heaven looks and feels like. It feels like having all your needs met right now. You don't have to immediately look to verify that this is being demonstrated. Just feel that your soul is loved beyond your mental comprehension and that you're at the center of the universe, because the center is everywhere and the circumference is nowhere. Everything is working together for your good right now. You are about your father-mother God's business of being on display for spirit. Feel that.

As you take on the spiritual practices of releasing the acquisitive nature, dropping opinions, complaints, and blame, and developing a non-reaction to circumstance, you'll begin to see life through new eyes. Heaven breaks out all over. You don't have to wait until you die. You just die to your narrowness, your lesser paradigm, that small point of view and myopic way of seeing the world. You walk strong and tall, saying, in substance, "My life is the life of God."

God is for you, and there is nothing against you. Let it sink in that you don't have to get anything to be happy. You have to let something if you want to live in bliss. To the world, it will look like you're getting more prosperous. It will appear as though you're getting healthier and that wonderful opportunities are coming in your direction. It'll look like that, but in reality, you're releasing an octave and an energy that is manifesting or becoming visible as opportunities, prosperity, and wholeness.

Divine spirit will have the space to move through you, articulating itself uniquely as poise and confidence, beauty and prosperity, safety and protection. There's nothing to hinder it, because, in this moment, you've entered into heaven. You've altered your point of view. You don't have to wait for anyone's else's permission to do this. You don't have to invite an external authority into your life to make you whole. You can give yourself permission to enter heaven on earth, right now.

One Day In Heaven

Take a breath right here
And we're going to move into a
prayerful moment right now
Take a breath right here
And then you ask, "How can
I bring value?
What's my job here?"
Sometimes your job may just be to pray
So we're here to wake up to this
awareness
And to allow for our life to be a
living demonstration
Of that which has never been born
and will never die

Now, feel all of your needs met right now
Just feel it, you can feel it
You don't have to immediately look
to see if it's demonstrating
Just feel it
Just feel that you're so loved
Beyond your mental comprehension
You're at the center of the Universe
Because the center is everywhere and
the circumference is nowhere
So you're at the center of the Universe
And you're just so loved right now

Everything is working together
for your good right now
You are about your Father-Mother-
God's business right now
To be on display for the Is-ness,
the Now-ness, and Forever-ness of
the Spirit now
Just feel that
We're describing Heaven

One day in Heaven
A day in ever-expanding good
That's Heaven
Just a day, one day in Heaven
So we're here to wake up into
a day in Heaven

And of course when we speak
of Heaven
We're not speaking of a far-off
state someplace that you go
to when you die
We speak of you becoming more
authentic, more alive, more awake
And the world is literally transformed
As individuals become more awake

In other words, happiness does not come from circumstances
Being the way you want them to be
The world of phenomena does not have your happiness,
your joy, nor your peace
That comes from Heaven
And Heaven is not a place, it is a state of consciousness
And if you want to really change the world
Wake up!

One day in Heaven, a day in ever-expanding good
That's Heaven
Just a day, one day in Heaven
And you will be guided
To be an answer, to be a solution
To be an energetic vibration of beauty and love

Take a breath right here
There are practices that allow us
To stay in this progressive dimension of consciousness
Those particular practices, when focused upon
Will allow us to be in Heaven all of the time
So a day in Heaven begins with this:
Notice and release your acquisitive nature
That part of you that wants to get something to be happy
Instead shift your awareness and ask the question
"How can I bring value to these individuals

that are coming into my life?"
Now if you take that on as a practice
Heaven breaks out all over
Now you're finding yourself in Heaven
Oh, just think of that word
Heaven, paradise

If you want to enter into Heaven
Just take one day of letting go
Of your acquisitive appetite
Just want to take one day, one day
Acquisitive appetite: in check
Opinions: in check
Complaining: in check
Blaming: in check
And then learn one day to just develop
A kind of a non-reaction to phenomena of apparent negativity

You're here to dispense the divine gifts
Not to get anything
And when you step into that space
And you decree something
It will manifest, because you are not out of alignment
With the fundamental order of existence!

6 In This Love Together (PART 1)

We want to rise high
And we have to see it to be it
We have to see that
Begin to see with the eye behind the eye
Hear with the ear behind the ear
Feel with the heart behind the heart
So that you can see the invisible
Hear the inaudible
Do the impossible

We walk a spiritual path seeking to activate the mystery lodged within the sacred spaces between our cells that bespeak of infinite possibility. That primordial void becomes activated when we say yes to life. In that dynamic moment, something unprecedented begins to happen. You to begin to see with the eye behind the eye, hear with the ear behind the ear, and feel with the heart behind the heart—so that you can see the invisible, hear the inaudible, and do the impossible. The presence of God becomes evident everywhere. Even in the midst of calamity, disease, disharmony, or scarcity, life invites you to step into the high vibration that allows for the infinite presence of God to have its way with you.

Getting in step with God may mean falling out of step with society. But the truth is, we don't necessarily want to fit in to a high tech-low touch society anyway. We don't want to fit into a society that is becoming increasingly shallow. Modern society exalts celebrity, while it denigrates character.

We don't want to fit into a society that's number one in heart attacks, cancer, and the building of prisons. We want to rise higher. So rather than strive to fit into society's definition of success, let's instead become creatively maladjusted. Let's be in the vanguard of that which is seeking to emerge, that which wants to express in, through, and as each and every one of us. As we evolve, we come to an understanding that the eternal qualities of God operate on a very different level than our manufactured personalities, which are artifacts of the ego. The ego is concerned with fitting in, being liked, admired, and praised; and making whatever adjustments to itself that are required to earn society's approval. But character is something else. Character is that part of God that's etched on your soul. Character is a repository for love, compassion, humility, creativity, kindness, and joy. Personality, on the other hand, conforms to the world.

We want to wake up so that we literally become transformers of the collective consciousness on the planet through the delivery of our gifts, talents, and skills. Every individual on this planet is a fully franchised expression of infinite potential and divine possibility, and when we unleash it in our lives the world transforms. Enlightened beings create enlightened societies.

When you study the history of people like Gandhi, Martin Luther King, Jr., Mother Teresa, and other great contributors to the world, you find that some of them didn't necessarily have pleasing personalities. That's not why we love them. We don't give out Nobel Peace Prizes to people because of their pleasing personalities. They had a depth of character that forced something life-changing into expression. They walked in the direction of their vision and manifested something of benefit to society. Each of us is empowered to do the same in some aspect of life. Age is not a factor, the color of one's skin is not a factor, education is not a factor, your zip code is not a factor. There's something within you that is greater than any of the outer details of your life, and it's begging for expression through you.

Consider the teaching of Jesus the Christ recorded in Matthew 6:19, "Do not store up for yourselves treasures on earth... but store up for yourselves treasures in heaven, where neither moth nor rust consume and where thieves do not break in and steal. For where your treasure is, there your heart will be also." We know that heaven is not a place we go to when we die. We know that heaven is the realm of evolutionary progress, of ever-expanding good. It is the edge of our growth as we constantly evolve into our true selves. Laying up treasures in heaven means expanding our consciousness to hold the divine ideas that are in the mind of God, that they may express through us.

I want you to take seriously the law described in the Bible which says that to he or she who has, more shall be given. He or she who has not, even that which they have shall be taken away. The wisdom of that scripture is the revelation that we have everything that we need within. We lack nothing. From a spiritual perspective, we can speak of "need" as something within us that needs to express itself. When you wake up every day saying, "I've got so much to give. I've got so much to live. I've got so much to express," the law corresponds and that which you need begins to pour into expression as guidance, support, and tangible supply—everything that is required to fulfill your purpose on the planet. But if you wake up each day saying, "Oh, I don't have enough to get by. I don't have enough money. I don't have enough resources. I don't have enough time," then universal law responds, "Even that which you have will be taken away," because you're cursing that which has already been given.

Not that it isn't anything personal. It's simply the way the law operates by corresponding to the nature of your song, your life's mantra. It corresponds to the vibration you emanate. So when you're laying up treasures in heaven, you're actually expanding your point of view and embracing the spiritual ideas that are proliferating in the universe. When you embrace this truth with gratitude, the law begins to work on your behalf. Goodness and mercy follow you all the days of your life, meaning that all the errors that you've made become null and void the moment you come into alignment with the wholeness of God. Those mistakes are turned into stepping-stones to a greater opportunities to grow, develop, and unfold.

There are some strategies that we can begin to apply in order to make our consciousness available for our gifts to freely express. One is to stop saying everything that we think and instead start thinking about everything that we say. In other words, to create a gap by pausing before what were thinking comes out of our mouth. If you tend to suffer from foot-in-mouth disease, not only will you be healed, you'll also find yourself saying that which is true, beautiful, uplifting, inspiring, and healing. Your communication will build bridges rather than walls. You'll begin to see that there's a dimension of your ego that is speaking just to be heard, that wants to be right and liked.

When you begin to think before you speak, your words will become more powerful and have a potent impact. You're not just talking because you're uncomfortable with silence. You're listening to something deeper within, and when you do speak, your words carry the vibration of compassion, upliftment. The things you decree through the spoken word manifest. The power that comes through the words spoken over your tongue, as well as under the tongue, are potent. So before you speak, just give the words a preliminary test. Are they kind? Are they necessary? Are they true?

If you follow this prescription, do you know what will happen? You'll find that you're comfortable with silence, that in that silent space creativity will start to brew, intuition will be activated. You'll notice that your ideas aren't a rehash of the same ideas you had before. Original ideas will flow, popping in whenever you finally give your mind and your mouth a break. So allow some space to catch an idea, a song, a poem, prose, a new ways of doing business, sharing and shining. These expressions have an opportunity to come through when you shut up and listen for a moment. You've got two ears and one mouth, and there's probably a reason.

The next strategy is to practice thinking from a creative awareness rather than from a competitive one. What does that mean? If you observe your mind, you'll discover that throughout the course of the day you not only compare yourself to other people, your actions are based on what others may think and how they will respond to you. You create a plan for how you're going to live your life based on comparisons to other people, rather than catching yourself and beginning again from a creative point of view.

For example, during the real-estate crisis, those who knew anything about it suddenly became experts in terms of how bad it was and that no one was making any money on real estate. That "fact" became a predominating belief. Therefore, many people sat around making no money and commiserating with one another about it. The fact is, there were a lot of people making money, because they didn't buy into that belief. Why? Because they chose to live creatively, on the edge of innovation. They opened themselves and experienced new opportunities.

When you deal with the presence of God that leads, guides, and directs you into compelling right action, you become an innovator. You become a co-creator with the infinite presence of God, and that never runs dry. There's no scarcity in it. Seek to prove that law in your life. If you want to be free in the Spirit, don't take your lead from the external world.

Remember the story about the hundredth monkey? A female monkey started to wash her yams in water. This was notable, because monkeys normally eat the yams rather than clean them first. Pretty soon a few other monkeys started washing their yams. After a while, when a certain number of monkeys had adapted this behavior, the monkeys on an island miles away spontaneously began to wash their food before eating it. This phenomenon was called the hundredth monkey theory. When so many people become involved in a certain practice or dynamic, there's a sudden evolutionary leap in the collective consciousness where multitudes of persons begin practicing the same thing. What isn't talked about is the fact that 40 percent of the monkeys didn't change their habit. In our society, that 40 percent would be largely represented by individuals who were successful doing things in certain ways, kept applying those models of success, and as a result became stuck.

Another thing that doesn't get talked about is the very first monkey to wash his yams. The first monkey represents a person who is creatively maladjusted, who's willing to do something in a way it's never been done before. What the world needs is individuals who aren't afraid to try something new, who aren't just stuck in practices of the past, doing the same things over and over again. Opportunities to innovate and create open up when you become aware that you are one with the creative nature of Spirit.

Competitive thinking won't necessarily help us access this new way of being. Next, resist the urge to jump into water-cooler conversations about the gossip and trends of the moment. Such a habit can lead to what you discuss becoming a part of your belief system, otherwise known as BS. You want to strike down the tyranny of trends by telling yourself the truth that: God is all there is. God is the source and substance of my supply. Though I walk through the valley of the shadow of lack and limitation, the valley of the shadow of death, the valley of the shadow of seeming not-enoughness, I will not fear. This is laying up treasures in heaven.

The third step is to accept that somewhere within you is a genius waiting to express. Some people have a little difficulty with this. Some of you are operating under a belief system that was born out of someone else's opinions back in junior high or high school. Someone said that you weren't smart enough, that you were slow, that you had a low IQ or nonsensical lies like that. You've been carrying around false perceptions of yourself, incorrectly believing that genius and IQ have something to do with each other. In reality, genius and IQ have nothing in common. IQ is simply the measure of one's capacity to comprehend symbols and words. It cannot measure genius, and it's certainly not the measure of success.

There are so many different kinds of genius. Genius means you have a particular gift of creative expression that you've honed so beautifully, so magnificently, that when people look at it and look at you, they are uplifted, inspired, challenged in a positive way. Genius lives within you, so take on that vibration as a fact of your individual existence. Jesus, Buddha, Krishna—they were spiritual geniuses. Ask yourself: "What kind of genius am I? Wherein does my genius lie?" When you ask this question with sincerity, a response will be given.

Release any self-imposed boundaries. Look for evidence of the genius within yourself and others. Appreciate what you see. Let go of any boundaries, even if just for a moment, that keep you from being a lover of humanity. Remember these words of the mystical theologian Dr. Howard Thurman: "You cannot love humanity in general. You can only love humanity in particular. You can only love humanity by loving the people around you, the people that you see every day, the people you meet on the street."

There are some people who walk into a room and their vibration is "Here I am." And then there are other people that walk into a room giving off the vibration of "There you are!" The magnificent energy with which they meet other people is: "There you are! You're beautiful. I'm here to support you. I'm here to love you. I'm here to bless you. I'm here to support you. There you are." That's the kind of consciousness we want to birth within ourselves and practice with all who cross our path.

Remember, you and all beings are vehicles for the living intelligence that governs the universe. You want to develop a beginner's mind, which is childlike in nature, allowing for the universe to take over your life so that nothing becomes impossible for you. Then you want to release any inhibitions where love, kindness, and generosity of the heart are concerned so that when you walk into a room you bring the vibration of there you are! Then there is a secret, sacred, silent blessing that happens simply because you've walked in the room and realize that we're all in this love together.

Do you realize that you are a reflection of the entire universe, that the space between the very cells of your body temple replicate the space between solar systems? As within, so without. All of the power that births galaxies and solar systems at thousands of miles a minute, that same power is within you. Choose in this moment to activate it. The talents and the capacities within you are waiting to be delivered as only you can deliver them. Walter Russell once said that mediocrity is self-inflicted and genius is self-bestowed. Bestow the genius code upon yourself. Don't wait for anybody's permission. Give it to yourself right now. Let the living intelligence of God move through you. From this moment forward, live your life in this octave.

In This Love Together (PART 2)

As the Buddha described
"Once you hear the Truth, its not going to rest
until it becomes fully available in your awareness."
There are some blessings happening in your life
And you don't even know about them yet
There are some blessings happening
Begin by counting the ones you can see

The visible universe is a manifestation of Spirit's beauty, infinite nature, and lawful order which fuel the evolutionary progress of our third-dimensional world. As a spiritual being having a human incarnation, you are a recipient of this life energy and a participant in universal law. In the same way, as you release the life energy which animates your life, you also set your evolutionary unfoldment in motion.

We are meant to evolve into our highest potential. Whatever it is that you've accomplished up to this moment, whatever level of success you've attained, the trickster ego seductively whispers, "I did it. I've made it!" while the spirit within says, "Good start!"

That is the nature the soul's evolution. It sweeps you up on a sacred quest, an adventure to uncover more of your authentic self. There's always something else to discover because you're an individualized manifester of your cosmic destiny. The holy pilgrimage is to go within yourself. The sacred ground lies beneath your feet. There's never an end point to be reached in our growth and development.

In releasing the gifts of your divine inheritance, your life becomes a continuation of spirit in that you have come from the invisible realm to give expression to your spiritual capacities in the realm of the physical, including all that is contained in the human experience. Sometimes this means that we discover the gifts contained in the crises that manifest in our lives. Now you don't want to blow a good crisis, especially a good, juicy one. Even when you agonize over the circumstances wondering, how am I going to get out of this? My back is against the wall. I'm at my wit's end. I don't see a way out. This has never happened before. Oh, my God!

These kinds of crises are the best ones. When they come along, it means that you're going to have an opportunity for rapid growth—if you accept the challenge to evolve by giving up habitual patterns, beliefs, opinions, and other sabotaging baggage. Most of us have such heavy baggage we've been tripping on throughout our lives. A good crisis can help you give up all that baggage in a relatively short period of time. Why? Because inside you really know that time's up and you have to let your cherished habit go. Your higher self and the universe have conspired to put yourself in a position where change is essential.

If you study the world of aphids, you'll see that these insects will go to a particular bush and multiply. They'll eat all of the leaves off the bush and right when the food has run out, they sprout wings and fly away in search of more food. But that doesn't happen until the food is gone. Like these and other species in nature, we have this same capacity. The difference is that we don't do it instinctually; we have to choose to evolve. We have to participate in our own evolution by saying yes to it.

Human beings don't operate on an instinctual level. Intuition, volition, and willingness also play pivotal roles in our growth. We can think independent of circumstances, and therefore have the ability to participate in that which is trying to evolve through us. We begin that process by blessing and being grateful for whatever crisis we face, because a challenging crisis compels us into a greater degree of right action in our lives.

Our breakdowns really are breakthroughs. Old habits, thought patterns, belief systems, and outdated ways of doing things are given the opportunity to be eliminated from your life. As the old ways fall apart, new paradigms come into being. The moment we try to stop remain stagnant—which occurs when we're comfortable with our habits—we enter into the different hell realms. Hell is a state of consciousness called stagnation. On the other hand, the moment we say yes to the challenges and blessings that come into our lives, we enter heaven, which is the realm of ever-expanding good.

When we look at relationships we can realize that, "It's not a breakup to makeup; it's a breakup to wake up before we make up." You're in the process of waking up to deep and abiding self-love, compassion, forgiveness, and appreciation. You're waking up to a magnificent inner vision for your life. You're waking up to how significant you are and entering to a conscious "at-one-ment" with the beloved. In the physical realm, your beloved may be your business partner, a relative, friend, or significant other. In any case, you're not two halves coming to make a whole, but two wholes coming together in a wholly holy way. Through this dynamic, you're able to dissolve drama from your lives. If you experience an upheaval in your romantic relationship, you can forego the drama of: Oh, please come back! I need you. I can't live without you. What am I going to do without you? You're going to live! That's what you're going to do.

There's a glorious vision inside of you that's trying to emerge, to express in, through, and as you. When you enter into that vibration, you find yourself in harmony with like-minded individuals, beaming the light of Spirit. Together, you shine it, share it, and circulate it. This is your life on God consciousness.

When there's a breakdown where the body temple is concerned, it is a moment for us to become aware that we are more than the physical. Indeed, the body temple is just that: the temple of the living Spirit. The body temple is simply the vehicle through which we reveal and communicate the love, peace, joy, wisdom, and our unique vision for being here on the planet. When you begin to realize that, the body temple responds.

It's common for us to want to be healed of whatever illness, disease, or injury we're facing. Sometimes, when an individual has asked for prayer for the healing of their body temple, I ask, "Why do you want to be healed? What are you going to do once you get your body functioning? Oftentimes, the person can't tell me. Why be healthy if you're not going to allow a great vision to take over your life?

When there's a breakdown in the body, ask yourself, "Who am I? What is trying to express through me?" Then let your spirit within answer you, because it will! As its answers to these questions pour into your awareness, you'll begin to live for something bigger than your little self, for more than your body, than the physical. Then the body may become aligned with that vision and flexibility, and recovery, rejuvenation, and regeneration occur.

When there's a breakdown in your financial aspect of life, in the area of right livelihood, it means that on some level you've been depending on that which you can see, and the universe is inviting you to now understand that divine substance and supply is yours from the invisible side of life. The universe is asking you to have a breakthrough into this awareness, so that you can begin to live from the manna from heaven consciousness. The universe is saying, "What you are being invited to do is to pause and create a space in those areas of your life that don't seem to be working so that insight can enter, so that you can release the toxins of animosity, guilt, shame, hate, projection, and resentment. As you do, then love, compassion, wisdom, clarity, forgiveness, peace, and kindness will fill that space.

If you want to create space where the body temple is concerned, you might consider—after checking with your health provider—to fast one day a week. On the first day of your fast, place your attention on how the Spirit's life energy is sustaining you and give thanks. Creating this space causes fresh, vitalized energy to flow throughout your body temple, and you will observe how you are living directly from life force.

In the area of supply, you create a space by sharing, giving, tithing, investing, and circulating your financial resources. As you may have read in that little book, *Living from the Overflow,* we don't believe in spending anything. We don't want to spend time with anybody. We don't want to spend money. Why? Because anything that is spent is gone. Instead, circulate the energy of money, love, kindness, professional gifts, talents, and skills. In everything that you do, see it from the framework of circulation. When you circulate energy, nothing is lost, nothing is spent. Because it's been put into circulation, it will circulate back to you! Out of the blue, someone you don't even know may give you money, which is the money you circulated coming back to you. When you give, serve, and circulate, the energy of abundance is going to find you. It's going to track you down. Goodness and mercy won't just follow you, they're going to track you down and tackle you.

Coming back to the subject of crises, know that they are opportunities to expand yourself into greater expression. Being an expression of God, yours is a destiny of a greater expression of beauty, joy, and creativity in your life. I'm talking about the presence of God, which is the same yesterday, today, and forever. It never compromises itself, it is never fickle, and its nature is unconditional love.

Wherever we look in society, we can see things breaking down. Structures that don't serve the vibration of the planet, that aren't in keeping with the integrity and harmony of the universe, have got to break down. They give way to new structures being funded which function at a higher level of integrity, love, and creativity. For example, currently the breakdown of global warming is leading to a breakthrough of green, sustainable living. But unlike the aphid, the collective society has to choose this vision in order to experience it.

Another example is that when we give service in our communities, we're choosing to fund a vision of a better life. When we meditate, we're choosing expand our awareness, our mindfulness. When we're praying, we're choosing to uplift, heal, and transform ourselves and the world. What and whom will you serve: God or materialism? God or ego? The eternal or the transitory?

Each and every one of us is a reflection of the image and likeness of the divine. The Spirit's name is written across our brow. Even when we act contrary to our true nature, its image and likeness is still in tact. It still recognizes as it's own, even when we don't recognize ourselves. So when the crises and the breakdowns come, it's Spirit's way of saying, "Can you hear me now? Ah, you are hearing me now!"

Place your attention in your heart center. Take a breath. Close your eyes, and focus on the awareness that the law of your life is in harmony with the presence of God. You may have been living your life concerned with what others are thinking about you. You may have been playing the game of being superior or inferior to them, or trying to impress them. Release such notions, and in this moment live in an awareness that Life is for you, it is mothering you, and there is no need for superiority or inferiority. Let the inner spirit within your soul be the source of your insights, wisdom, intelligence, and transforming knowledge—all that has already been given to you by divine inheritance. Allow your inner eye to see that you're surrounded by divine substance, divine good. It is everywhere. Say to yourself, "I give thanks for everything. I live in pure gratitude. I am receptive to my good. I am available to the all-good of Spirit."

Brother Lawrence, the 17th-century Christian monk, was asked how he'd been able to maintain such a heightened state of awareness of his oneness with God. He replied, "I gave up all that was not he [meaning God] and I began to live in the world as if only he and I existed. As if only God and I existed." He could say this because he was consciously choosing to live in such a way, and he exerted the spiritual discipline to enter that state of consciousness, a consciousness of oneness with God. Court that kind of awakening in your own life. Know that it is possible to live in this world as if only God exists, because it's true. God exists as you. God exists as the people around you. God exists as opportunities that open up for you. You can choose not to see anything other than this. Let it speak to you throughout your day, then it will be present in your dream stage, it will pour out through your poetry, your song, your dance, your every movement.

As the Buddha described, once you hear the truth, it's not going to go away. You've heard the truth and, one way or another, at one time or another, you will fully awaken to the awareness that your life is the life of the divine, that you are already an enlightened being.

You may resist this truth, you may deny it for a while, but it's going to keep working on you, keep revolving within you, just as it is in this very moment, whether you are aware of it or not. Whatever has brought you to the point of awareness in which you find yourself today is the same thing that seeks to express itself in, through, and as you fully and completely. It's emerging now, and soon you will sprout some wings and fly into the undiscovered region of your infinite potential.

Breathe into that awareness, feeling yourself connected to and blessed by it. The grace of God is pouring over you. Sometimes we don't even know how blessed we are. There are blessings happening in your life that you don't even know about yet. Sometimes blessings come disguised and we say, "Oh no! I don't want that! That isn't what I've been praying for!" But right within that disguised blessing is something our soul is prepared to welcome or it wouldn't have arrived at the threshold of our life, of our awareness.

So begin to count not only the blessings you can see, of which you are aware, but also give thanks for those you can't yet see. Say to yourself, "My life is magnificent in every way—the good, the harmony, the love, the creativity, the joy, the harmony—are beyond my imagining! I am so humbly grateful for life, and to Life itself!"

This is your life on God. This is your brain on love. This is your mind on peace. This is your being on creativity. This is your body temple on vibrant health. All of this and more is who and what you are.

In This Love Together

Take a breath
As the Buddha described
"Once you hear the Truth, it's not going to rest
Until it becomes fully available in your awareness"

There are some blessings happening in your life
And you don't even know about them yet
There are some blessings happening
Begin by counting the ones you can see

You're the spiritual image and likeness of the presence
Take a breath right here
We are here to hold the space
Where we're beginning to really see that
The presence of God is everywhere, everywhere

We want to rise high
And we have to see it to be it
We have to see that
Begin to see with the eye behind the eye
Hear with the ear behind the ear
Feel with the heart behind the heart
So that they can see the invisible
Hear the inaudible
Do the impossible
There are some blessings happening

It's just too good
It's too good, this is too good!
My life is just too good
The love is just too good
My blessings are just too good
The harmony is just too good
My life is just too good
Prosperity is just too good
The love is just too good
Oh, it's just too good

We're in this joy together
We're in this peace together
Oh, yes! Oh, yes!
We're in this Love together

We want to rise high
And we have to see it to be it
We have to see that
Begin to see with the eye behind the eye
Hear with the ear behind the ear
Feel with the heart behind the heart
So that they can see the invisible
Hear the inaudible
Do the impossible

7   Energetic Shapeshifter

When you begin to take a stand
In your own life
The idea is to no longer run
From those areas of your life
That you are not happy about
Might even be embarrassed about
Shift that energy
Into the area that doesn't seem to be working well
Now you're a candidate for insight
For revelation, Divine guidance
Now you're a candidate for compelling right action
Will you be made whole?

Take a moment to stop and feel the power of God cascading over you. Allow yourself to be sensitive to the fact that you're living, moving, and having your beingness in an energetic field saturated with the love of God. That's a revolutionary perspective: the power of God that you feel all around you, and all through you, is the very essence of your life. This grand power, this love-intelligence, is seeking to break into conscious awareness of itself as you. In taking on this perspective, you're no longer subject to the idea that you're cut adrift from a reluctant deity who periodically throws out blessings depending on whether or not you've followed the right rules.

Indeed, every impulse that you have to love, give, and share, to be compassionate, bold, or generous, is the impulse of God itself seeking expression. As you enter into that kind of spiritual understanding, you cut your moorings away from any sense of victimization: They did this to me. When are they going to stop doing this to me? The universe has done this to me. God has done this to me! It becomes possible to release yourself from this victimhood mentality by stepping into the awareness that if God really is for you—and God is your life—then what can be against you? Nothing can be against you other than your perceptions, positions, opinions, and beliefs, which coagulate as the obstacles that continue to crop up in your life.

If God is for you, and there is nothing against you, you might as well give in and be great. You might as well give in and be happy. You might as well give in and be prosperous. You might as well give in and allow your life to bear witness to the excellence, the same excellence to which the elegance of the universe also bears witness. You might as well allow for your life to bear witness to the boldness, confidence, courage, and beauty that's trying to express itself through and as you.

Accepting these insights as true means no longer allowing one area of our life to be in excellence while other areas of our life remain below par. Instead, we're called to stand on the conviction that we're the renaissance men and women of our age. We no longer look to others to see greatness in action, but step up to the plate to be the social, spiritual artists of our time.

Thus, we've come into the awareness that we can become energetic shape-shifters. The practice of energetic shapeshifting, as it's taught by many indigenous cultures, involves placing your attention on an area of your body, or an area of your life, that's in excellent condition. Then you allow yourself to experience tremendous gratitude as you contemplate that excellence, consciously feeling into the energy of it. Next, feel yourself transferring that energy into an area of your life that may not be operating so smoothly. Watch with your inner eye as the spiritual transmission takes place. The energy begins to speed up. The area of your life that had been stagnated begins to operate at a much higher level.

Everything is energy. Even the thoughts that you're having right now are units of mental energy that are measured in beta-frequencies (or alpha, theta, or delta). Every unit of energy in creation is oscillating, vibrating. The chair you're sitting on, the thoughts you're thinking—everything is in flux. By simply observing your life with an intention for transformation, an intention for growth, you change your whole life on the subatomic level. This is the principle behind the observer effect, which has been widely discussed by quantum physicists in recent years.

But so very often, our attention becomes fixated on the areas in life that we're unhappy or embarrassed about. We've judged these areas as being not up to snuff, and therefore they carry a kind of dense, emotional charge around them. Sometimes, when you think about these things (or circumstances or people), you get sad or depressed. It's quite normal to believe that the depression is coming from the issues associated with your area of concern. But, in fact, those thoughts and feelings are actually coming from previously held judgments that you have about yourself, which have downloaded and coagulated as a mood.

Depression becomes cyclical. It feels much easier to run away from problems that are uncomfortable or frightening. You do everything you can not to look at those areas. You go to a happy hour and pretend that you're happy. You overeat and put all kinds of white flour, sugar, and soft drinks (which aren't really soft) into your body. You watch television. You get on the phone and talk about people, but gossip is poison, so the person you've called gets tired, and you get tired of yourself. And then, at the end of the day, you're back with your stuff again. You've exhausted yourself by running away in all those different directions, and you still can't get rid of the issues. They're right there waiting for the first moment of quiet so they can pop back up and say, "Remember me?"

The idea is to no longer run from the areas of your life that you feel aren't working the way you want them to—whether the problems are emotional, mental, spiritual, or physical. Instead, place your attention on the vibration of the things that are in harmony in your life. Feel into them. Declare them. Be appreciative of them, thankful for them. As you shift that energy into the areas that don't seem to be working well, you'll feel the lower vibration begin to shift.

Now you're a candidate for insight and revelation. You have greater access to divine guidance, transforming knowledge, and compelling right action. You're able to do what's necessary to progress in life while remaining in league with the vibration of joy and greatness. Now the problematic areas have an opening to come into harmony with the vibration of a very high standard of excellence.

This is what it means to energetically shapeshift. You move beyond the theory of relativity into the law of "unitivity," understanding polarity as it is witnessed in the physical dimension. In other words, there are only graduated levels of a singular condition. Hot is not the opposite of cold; cold is merely the absence of heat. Darkness is not the opposite of light; it's the absence of light. There are no opposites, really. There's just one unified field that has graduations of the only thing that there is: God.

God is love, peace, harmony, and wholeness. It's possible to experience these spiritual qualities in their fullness only when you stop fighting and resisting what appears to be their opposites. Instead, take on the practice of energetic shapeshifting by invoking your affirmative prayer, meditation, contemplation, sacred service, spiritual study, and fellowship. Transcend the theory of relativity that would keep you boxed into a belief that your destiny is wrapped up in your conditions, circumstances, or heredity, because such a belief indicates that you'll never go beyond what your parents did, or what they gave you, energetically or hereditarily, which is a bunch of hogwash.

Set yourself free, even if your freedom appears to be craziness to those around you. You have to be kind of crazy to stay sane in this world, because this world is crazy. Our society, as it's depicted by our media, is much like those old comic-book strips where the superhero gets transported to bizarro world where everything is backward. When you look out upon the world, there's a lot of insanity going on that masquerades as normality. We fall victim to the tyranny of trends when we take the lowest common denominator of our society and allow that to become the standard-bearer. This happens frequently in our society. I recall reading a newspaper article where contractors and politicians were celebrating the fact that they'd signed an agreement to build more weapons of war. They might as well have said, "Whoopee! We get to build more tanks. We get to build more bombs. We get to find more ways to kill people. Goodie!" Building war implements is the penultimate of lack of creativity. It showcases a total inability to respond creatively to the changing realities of our world. These individuals were caught up in survival mentality, regardless of the fact that they were representing billion-dollar corporations to the extent that they'd do anything to make money. To someone who has completely stepped out of that mind-set, it appears absolutely insane. These thought forms of lack, limitation, and scarcity interrupt everything.

On the other end of the spectrum are the companies and individuals who are evolving to reflect an evolved, forward-thinking consciousness. A number of years ago, IBM used to have signs that said, "Buyer Beware." Then Walter Russell and some other like-minded individuals got involved and shifted the entire dynamic at the company toward quality and service. Business used to be solely about the bottom line—profit. Now, many businesses are evolving to the point where their bottom line is about service.

When we don't evolve, we become trapped in bizzaro thinking and all of the havoc that it creates. Thoughts of separation, scarcity, lack, and limitation break into relationships. People enter into Bob-Barker-let's-make-a-deal kind of relationships: "Well, I'll bring 50 percent to the table if you bring your 50 percent to the table." People negotiate like they're commodities, as if love can be given and received in that kind of way. It's seen as normal. It's not normal, of course. It's not real; rather, it's realistic. You want to be real. You want to be an authentic being that grows into expressing love, compassion, honesty, and generosity, regardless of prior conditioning. You want to respond to the world from a state of loving compassion, regardless of what anybody else is doing in their relationship toward you. You're still being you, because your karma is not determined by how someone else treats you. Your karma is determined by how you treat them. Relationship is not about a 50-50 thing; it's two grown beings giving 100 percent of themselves every moment that they can, becoming conscious when they fall, and choosing to get back up to give 100 percent all over again.

To believe otherwise is to get stuck in limitation. Rather than breeding growth and elevation, these thought forms breed wars, rumors of wars, and that type of consciousness. Such a mentality begins to dissolve when you take a stand in your own life. Again, other people may think you're kind of crazy. In Rwanda, for example, where a tremendous genocide took place years ago, there's a whole movement championing love and forgiveness. People are working side-by-side with individuals whose families murdered their families during the genocide. They are seeking to use love to rebuild their country. There are many people in the world who see this approach—which is rooted in love and radical forgiveness—as crazy. They say, "I don't get it. These people were actually hating each other for years. They were killing each other for years, and now they're working side by side to build a new country?"

In a word, yes. The Rwandans have taken their lead, of course, from Nelson Mandela, who sanctioned forgiveness tribunals rather than the war tribunals. In doing so, he led his countrymen into an entirely different phase of human evolution. That's the kind of crazy we want to be! We want to be so crazy that we burst into sanity. We want our loving, generosity, and compassion to make history. You want people to look back at you and say, in substance, "There lived someone that loved so deeply, that gave so sincerely, that was so generous with their time and talents. They were so creative. They were so available to the Spirit. They held nothing back and literally changed the landscape and the mindscape of the human dimension of reality."

Living from this space is absolutely possible. It invites us to fall madly in love with the presence of God and to fall madly in love with one another ("each" other means one-to-one; one another means everyone) as emanations of God. We release ego-based ethnocentricity, which tries to convince us that someone who lives on the other side of the planet is different from us. We're all on this planet together, all astronauts on planet Earth, moving around the sun and our solar system, unfolding and evolving forever. We want to embrace that truth and fall madly in love with one another to the degree that it's history making.

Interestingly enough, every great movement or transformation that has happened in any culture around the planet happened through small groups of people being on the cutting edge of the emerging consciousness. Look back at the Berlin Wall falling; look at the end of apartheid; look at lunch counters being desegregated. When you examine these historical events, you'll see that they had nothing to do with governments; rather, they had everything to do with individuals and small groups of people who made inner changes, who spoke the truth, who prayed, who took action, who walked in the direction of their intentions. In response, outdated institutions crumbled, walls fell down, apartheid dissolved. Then governments reconfigured themselves around the change that had taken place within the citizenry.

You want to be crazy sane. You want to be as crazy as Jesus when he said, "Forgive them, for they know not what they do," knowing full well they knew exactly what they were doing. You want to be as crazy as the Buddha. You want to be as crazy as Mother Teresa when she said, "I see Christ in everybody, and I'm going to feed as many people as I possibly can." That's craziness. A whole life of service? Oh, that's nuts! Giving all the time? Oh, lord! You'll hear so many people say, "I just want to make some money. Give me a Coke and a smile. Let me OD on some sugar. Give me a cow and I'll kill myself faster than necessary by eating too much dead meat. (I'm sorry if these statements give offense to anyone. The truth is, my job is not just to comfort the afflicted, but also to afflict the comfortable.)

The world wants mad lovers of humanity to rise up with boldness in their love, compassion, and giving. As you go to and from your place of employment, your home, visiting with friends, and communicating with individuals with whom you come in contact, you want to ask yourself, "Where can I stretch myself today? Where have I been holding back? Where have I been living in mediocrity? Where have I been trying to not rock the boat?" And then you may have to send out a few memos: "I don't want to participate in gossip anymore. Can we go somewhere else for happy hour? Can we just meditate? Can we get together and do a visioning, a strategic plan for our life, and how it's going to be a lot better? How we can give more in the world? Can we use our time a little bit better?"

Stretch your awareness and ask yourself where you've capitulated and conformed to the world, this crazy Bizarro place, which is a reflection of the thoughts of lack, limitation, scarcity, and not-enough-ness. How can you choose instead to live in the field of plenitude and abundance, where all needs are met, where creativity and infinite possibility are birthed within your own soul?

Ask yourself where you can stretch, and suddenly the universe gets to become conscious of itself as your life in that specific area. God is everywhere. Again, we're not talking about an anthropomorphic being. We're talking about the presence of love, intelligence, beauty, elegance, and order that's conscious of itself everywhere and that has no withholding in it. Because you're created in its spiritual image and likeness, made from its divine substance, you have the capacity to permit that realization to take form in your awareness. Only you can be you. This universe does not repeat itself. Infinity keeps birthing and recreating itself, and it has created you for the specific purpose of revealing its full nature in, through, and as you.

In other words, you possess the full spectrum of everything that God is. There's absolutely nothing missing in you at all. Place yourself into an inner condition where there's a tuning-fork vibration to match that insight. Strike the chords within you that, heretofore, may never have been struck. Then something inside you will say, "Oh, this feels good. Wow, I remember this. I haven't felt this way since I was a kid. I had unlimited possibility. I thought I could do anything. What happened?"

When you strike the chord of possibility, your vibration changes from, "Guess what happened to me" to "This is who I am!" Eventually, you reach a point where you're able to hold the space of this high vibration. You find that you're able to hold it at your place of employment, in your relationships, on the freeway, and in the parking lot. You become willing to stretch, even if you stand out, even if you look crazy. I was talking to a woman in our community at Agape, who told me that after she did her taxes the accountant kept saying, "You're giving too much to your church." She told him, "Oh no, no, I tithe." And he said, "But you don't have to give that much. I can show you a way that you don't have to give that much and you could still get just as much back." She replied, "No, no, this is my community. I want it to remain strong so I can go there." He insisted, "You don't have to do that." And finally she said, "I may have to change accountants, but I'm not going to stop tithing." To that the accountant replied, "Oh no, no, you should tithe. Definitely!"

The point isn't about tithing, although tithing is a wonderful thing. The point is that the accountant thought she was crazy in her giving. He thought she was crazy in her commitment. You want to find areas in your life and stretch so much in those areas that people think you're crazy. You want to forgive that deeply. You want to love that profoundly. You want to be so creative that people who are locked in a mediocre mind state will think you're a little nuts, just like they thought that the people in South Africa and Rwanda were a little nuts having forgiveness tribunals after they'd endured genocide, abuse, and oppression. But those individuals were able to remain conscious to an undeniable pull from the Spirit within toward an expanded awareness. They refused to fall back asleep; instead, they fell awake into love and forgiveness. That's the only way humanity is going to reflect its deep and sincere inner intentionality to be all that it is meant to be on the planet.

In this way, we can eliminate thoughts of scarcity and lack without moving into gross materialism. We can eliminate the thought of separation without moving into uniformity. We eliminate the belief that the presence of God is absent in this physical world and literally surrender to the spiritual dimension that is right here all the time. Great artists, mystics, poets, entrepreneurs, and others have seen the next level of human evolution. We want to be in that number. We want to be the history makers, the lovers of humanity, where true richness resides.

As we turn within, we feel our way into the Presence. Then something wonderful happens: full-dimensional living, energetic shapeshifting, crazy sanity. We get in league with the history makers of our time by recognizing the presence of almighty God. We're not imagining that this love is far away from us, but understanding that it's closer than our breathing and nearer than our hands and feet. It's right on the ground where we now stand, because it is our very life. When we shift our energetic frequency to this level, we can see that we're the right person, at the right time, in the right place, with all of the resources within us to take the next step in our evolution. We become dynamic lovers of humanity, creators of prosperity, and expressers of creativity. We move into a mind-set of compassion based on our sense of oneness with all beings. Compassion is the highest form of love in that it understands the lack of understanding in others and meets judgment with kindness.

The universe is conspiring for our freedom so that it can be free to be us in our fullness, wholeness. God wants your liberation so that it has another playground to play in. Give thanks for that. Shift your energy into that vortex of high appreciation for your life, for your breath, and allow this magnificence to unfold.

Energetic Shapeshifter

Will you be made whole?
Take a breath
And ask, "Where can I
stretch myself where I'm
holding back?"
Step up into the awareness
Take a breath
This Power, this Presence, this Love

Place your attention on the
vibratory field
Because as you know, everything
is energy
Even the thought forms that
you're having
Are units of mental energy vibrating
Energetically shapeshift
With your affirmative prayer
Your meditation
Your contemplation
Your sacred fellowship
And begin to set yourself free
To energetically shapeshift your life!

You might as well give in and be happy

You might as well give in and be great
You might as well give in and be prosperous
You might as well, you might as well

When you begin to take a stand
In your own life
The idea is to no longer run
From those areas of your life
That you are not happy about
Might even be embarrassed about
Shift that energy
Into the area that doesn't seem
to be working well
Now you're a candidate for insight
For revelation, Divine guidance
Now you're a candidate for
compelling right action

Will you be made whole?
We're in the realm of ever-
expanding good
We enter now
Nothing can be against you
Other than your perception
You want to be an authentic being
Give in

8   Life Is Good

In you is such a Beauty and a Power and a Love
That can never die
It's always there, it's inviolate
And though it may be covered up by experience Temporarily
It's real and we are here to uncover that destiny
And allow it to shine according to our unique Patterns
As individual expressions of God

Everything we could want, hope for, or desire comes from divine consciousness through an avenue called awareness. Awareness allows us to see what's been given, provided, gifted to us by God. As we do our spiritual work, as we participate in our spiritual practices, we make ourselves candidates for expanded awareness. We enter the flow of preparing our minds, hearts, and souls to receive what's been gifted. The universal presence, the divine mind, withholds nothing. There's no off button in God. To better understand this phenomenon, think about electricity. Electricity is always electricity. It doesn't stop or start, although we have a linguistic expression which says, "I turned off the electricity today," when in fact we did not. While we may stop the electrical current from going to an appliance, we cannot stop the law of electricity itself from operating. Electricity is always flowing; it has always been itself.

In the same way, we can't stop God from being God. We can't stop love from being love. We can't stop beauty from being beauty. We can't stop joy and abundance from radiating. These are eternal qualities of God that are going to be expressed regardless of what we try to say or do about them. The only thing we can do is stop these spiritual qualities from flowing and expressing through our own individual life, whether we do so consciously or unconsciously.

You want to prepare yourself to gratefully receive that which is eternally being given. Have you heard the good news from the Bible that announced that, "It's God's good pleasure to give you the kingdom"? The presence of God ceaselessly gives, constantly radiates toward its creation. When a soul-opening occurs within you, when you yield and say yes to the Presence, you literally give joy to the spirit of God, because you have created a channel through which it may come into its own as you. You don't have to beg and plead with a reluctant deity to give you anything. It's the other way around. God is eagerly waiting for you to open up. Spirit is knocking at the door of you heart, asking, "Let me express through you! Let me sing and dance and create through you! Let me express my life through you! I don't want to be stuck in the abstract concepts. I don't want to be stuck in dogma. I don't want to be stuck in philosophical conversation. I want your heart! I've already given you mine! Set me free in your life!"

So let the prayer of your heart be to accept that which is eternally being given. This is the consciousness of receptivity and availability. You contain a vast amount of inherent wisdom within you, just as the acorn has within it all that is necessary to transform into a towering oak tree. Within your spirit there is an inherent knowing of the existence of excellence, brilliance, love, and joy, which is meant to be expressed in a way that is uniquely you. As you yield and say yes to this dynamic good that is trying to happen through you, that transformational knowing is activated.

Your sacred yes assists you in cultivating an energy of perpetual gratitude. This is not only a strategy, it's a practice. You're not going to automatically wake up happy and in gratitude every day. The ego is going to try to hold your mind hostage and rule the kingdom of your thoughts and perceptions on some days. Your mind is going to say, "What do you have to be grateful for? Are you out of your mind? You better try and understand what's really going on!"

Committing to a spiritual practice means hanging out in gratitude and thanksgiving, even when you don't feel like it. That's why it's called a practice. It's not enough to say, "Oh, today's a nice day and I'm happy. Oh, today's a bad day so I'm not in gratitude." If you're endeavoring to develop a skill or a talent, you get up and practice whether you feel like it or not. In order to live an excellent life and excel at what you love, in order for your soul to unfold and for you to gain the capacity to express that which is trying to come through you, the practice of gratitude is imperative. Live in this state of being until it takes over your life, because when you do, a great joy will take you over as you realize all that's waiting to articulate itself as your life experience.

It's interesting how bodily posture is a reflection of what's happening in the mind and heart. When resentment, worry, insecurity, and resistance to committing to growth and development occur, bodily posture reflects such choices. The mind is stuck, and the body reflects this through tightness and tension.

You want to allow yourself to enter into a state of mental, emotional, and physical acceptance, which means freedom. Give yourself permission to walk around in the privacy of your own home, assuming an open posture of receptivity. Begin to work from the physical all the way to the emotional and mental, and then the spiritual domain. Open up your arms up for a moment. Let yourself be receptive, and say out loud, "I'm available! I'm open to receiving my good. I'm completely available to receiving my good. I'm available to health, wholeness, prosperity, love, joy, and well-being. I accept it right here, right now."

You want to hang out in this kind of receptivity so that it flows through all aspects of your being. As you walk through your daily life, carry the vibration of availability and receptivity in your body, mind, heart, and spirit. Understand that this doesn't mean you're stopping to discern what serves your high resolve or doesn't. Being able to think independently is vital. However, most people move through their day without truly thinking; they're just rehashing the thoughts they had the day before, which is called mentation. When you remain open and available, insight, wisdom, transforming knowledge, and intuition begin to think through you. That's when mentation stops and real thinking begins. So don't cut off your mind. Use it rightly by being an avenue of awareness, truth, and excellence.

As you practice the art of living in gratitude, slowly add in the next phase of the strategy: mitigating fear. Fear is generated by the ego. The ego's job is to make you believe that you are a separate being cut off from everything and everyone else. A function of the ego is to assure that the human race continues to populate, so it let us know, "Hey, you're not a saber-toothed tiger. You are separate. Don't go wandering over there where the tigers are. You'll get eaten! From generation to generation, ego has passed down this perception of separation.

At this point in our evolution, the ego is still doing its job. It's still telling you that you're separate. It tells you that you're cut off from life and that you're cut off from God. The survival instinct that comes from the ego tells you to remain afraid in the face of the unknown. It wants to keep you in fear so you don't wander too close to anything threatening. When you buy into the egoic belief in separation, you forget that you're an eternal, immortal being who has never been born and will never die. This message overrides the awareness of your connection to the divinity within you. Believing that we're separate from everything has allowed us as a species to do all kinds of damage to one other and to the ecology of our planet. A sense of egoic fear and separation has made us forget our oneness with Mother Earth and our fellow human beings regardless of skin color, ethnicity, or sexual orientation. For the perpetuation of our sense of being a separate self, the ego casts a net of fear, doubt, and worry over us. Sadly, it's killing us.

We must transcend the ego so that the fear with which we've been programmed can begin to dissolve. When you're in fear, you can be controlled. Think about it—you cannot control an individual who's living in creativity, or who's receiving signals from the divine impulse of the Spirit. Such a person lives on the evolutionary edge of life.

Fear does not come from your heart; it comes from the surface mind influenced by ego. In the old days we used to say, "The devil made me do it. Beware of the devil!" Since God is omnipresent, there can't be God and something else, there can't be another autonomous power called the devil. What we used to call the devil is really a function of the egoic mind, the part of ourselves that is living separately, consciously or unconsciously turning off the electricity of discerning wisdom so that it can't flow through us. This is how the ego attempts to maintain its false power over us.

Mitigating fear is one of the reasons why we engage in daily prayer and meditation. Prayer and meditation allow us to bathe in the awareness of the presence of God. God is omniscient, omnipresent, omnipotent, and omni-active, being itself totally and completely in every moment. As we step into this awareness, healing occurs in our life. This is why we call it a revelation. This is why Ernest Holmes says, "There is nothing to heal, only something to be revealed."

Set an intention to stop living in fear. As Jesus the Christ said, "Fear not, little flock. It is your Father's good pleasure to give you the kingdom." Open up and let God express through you fully. Don't be afraid of the shadow. Understand that shadows are being caused by some blockage of the light within the soul. Turn toward the light for a greater understanding of your divinity. Let the shadows of doubt and death dissolve.

The next step in the practice is to stop hating others. You may be saying, "Well, I'm not a hater. I don't hate." I beg to differ with you, because there's something called pet peeve-ism. Pet peeves are things that we love to hate. When something goes wrong, when we see what we consider abhorrent behavior, or when we focus on the things that we don't like in the world, we find ourselves saying, "Oh, I hate that!" But Spirit says not to hate anyone or anything. Universal law doesn't know the difference between you hating something from a justified place or you hating something from an unjustified place. It only knows the vibration of hate. If you're a hater, you're blocking the flow of your own receptivity to the good of life.

When something unwanted, such as a feeling of hate, comes up in your awareness, take it as a sign that it's your time to pray, that it's time to have a conversation with Spirit. Perhaps you could bring to mind the example of Mohandas K. Gandhi and his refusal to hate the British colonists even as they severely abused the Indian population. You could think about Dr. King refusing to hate the racists who persecuted his race. Both Gandhi and King exhibited unconditional love and forgiveness, even though the systems they fought were, perhaps, something to be hated.

Be not a hater. Instead, be a lover of the divine Presence and all creation. Love is something that must be generated from within your being. Move through life with an intention to generate love everywhere you go, toward all beings who cross your path. Some people turn off their love switch and walk around saying, "I'm looking for love," or "I'm waiting for love. And I'm going to keep waiting for it. In fact, I've been waiting 36 years, and it still hasn't come yet, God!"

Don't look or wait for love. Generate it. Love has got to know your spiritual address before it can show up in your life. When you generate love, it's like the neon sign proclaiming, "I'm here, and I'm love! I live here, and I live in love!" Then, everywhere you go, companionship, right relationships, and loving friendships will unfold with grace and ease.

People who are living unconsciously don't want to be bothered with those who are conscious. Holding fast to your intention to love may make people say you're a bit weird. They may talk about you a little bit at work, which would probably sound something like this: "Don't try to gossip with her. She's not even going to listen to you. She's different..." Let them talk. Just remember to invoke this potent mantra when you discover that other people talking about you: "So what!"

As the sincerity of that "So what!" declaration flows through your heart and soul, you embody the vibration of that which you want to be. You make yourself a candidate for insight, a home where love, peace, joy, and contentment take up residence. Your world changes. The ego loses control. Any residue of fear and hate dissolves as you become a place of open receptivity for the presence of God. That vibration trumps every other vibration and allows you to become impervious to the slings and the arrows of this world. They can't touch you because you're not vibrating at their frequency.

Ask yourself if you are prepared to receive the vibration of the most high. This inner work is imperative so that your mind, heart, and soul are available channels for the good of God. The windows of heaven will be open, and the spirit of the living God will pour forth a blessing too big for you to receive. Again and again you will continue to expand in consciousness as a way of life.

There's an old story about a gentleman who walked around his town wearing a sandwich board. On the front of the sandwich board was written, "I am a fool." People were driving by staring at him while he stood there confidently radiating such life and luminosity. What passers by didn't know was that on the back of the sandwich board it said, "I'm a fool for God. Whose fool are you?"

Until we're ready to receive the vibration of the most high, we're ego's fool. Perhaps we've been fooled by the fear, doubt, and worry that runs amuck in the human experience. It's got us dangling on a string like a puppet. We're constantly afraid yet we don't really know why. Then we turn on the news to find out what's happening, maybe get some insight into why we feel so afraid. But that's not what you want to do.

It's time to wake up to the fact that you're what's happening. You're the news, the history maker. Wake up each day with an intention to receive the good that wants to happen through you. The Presence wants to shine, to give and to sing through you. The presence of God wants to create and heal through you. Are you available?

When you truly know who you are, you'll assume a receptive heart, accepting greatness as the intrinsic state of your being. And then you discover that the giving and the receiving become one thing. It's like a full breath. You can't have just an inhalation. You've got to have an exhalation, too. The trees want that exhalation, just as you inhale the gift of oxygen that the trees exude. Giving and receiving is one movement of the spirit through you. It's one breath, in and out.

Make yourself available to being the greatest giver and receiver that you can possibly be. Generate your good from within your own being. Everything you want, hope for, and desire is already here. Embodying this truth can change the world as you know it in the twinkling of an instant. You'll no longer be conformed to the world, but transformed by the renewing of your mind and heart.

This is our moment. God made no mistake when it wrote out the beautiful, unfolding pattern of light that we are. In fact, spirit gave us everything we need to release that light throughout eternity. It's a good and wonderful destiny. A beautiful destiny. Are you ready to live it?

Life Is Good

Life is good and all is well, yes? Yes!
Life is good and all is well, yes? Yes!
Can you feel it? Yes!
Life is good. Yes!
Can you feel it? Yes!
And all is well
Life is good, can you feel it? Yes!

In you is such a Beauty and a Power
and a Love
That can never die
It's always there, it's inviolate
And though it may be covered up
by experience temporarily
It's real and we are here to
uncover that destiny
And allow it to shine according
to our unique patterns
As individual expressions of God

So we are gonna go home now
We are letting go to the
all-creating Spirit
The all-creative Spirit, the
all-originating Spirit
That is totally giving of itself

totally and completely
At every point of the cosmos
Without any sense of withhold
whatsoever

Mm. Mm. Mm. Feel it.
Life is good. Yes!
Ain't God something? Mm. Mm. Mm.
Feel it? Something, something,
something. Mm. Mm. Mm.
Life is good
Mm. Mm. Mm.

Do you know who you are? Yes!
This Presence wants to live through you
Do you know who you are? Yes!
This Presence wants to give through you
Do you know who you are? Yes!
This Presence wants to sing through you
Do you know who you are? Yes!
This Presence wants to create through you
Do you know who you are? Yes!
This Presence wants to heal through you
Do you know who you are? Yes!
Do you know who you are? Yes!

Then you will assume the receptive posture
And accept the greatness that is
Trying to happen through you
I'm ready, I'm available, I am open
And then you discover something
This is our moment, this is our destiny
It's a good destiny
It's a wonderful destiny
God made no mistakes
When God wrote the beautiful, unfolding pattern of delight as You

Life is good and all is well, yes? Yes!
Life is good and all is well, yes? Yes!
Mm. Mm. Mm. Yes!

9   Mystic Cord Of Memory

(A note to the reader) Distinctly unique from the preceding eight chapters, "Mystic Cord Of Memory" is not a transcript of a talk. Upon emerging from his morning meditation session, in a spontaneous, mystical flow of consciousness, Michael Bernard Beckwith shares the intimate insights and revelations of his soul, which appear in the italicized song verses below. In the nonitalicized sections he expands upon how the individual human spirit, living in conscious oneness with the Ineffable, unfolds the mystery, beauty, and perfection of one's divine destiny.

> *I want to invite you on a sweet and wonderful journey*
> *It's a journey that you're already on*
> *But now you're going to embrace this journey more consciously*
> *This is the journey on which you are going to lengthen*
> *The cord of memory*
> *The mystic cord of memory*
> *You are going to come back to yourself*
> *You are going to remember who and what you are*
> *And have a joyful reunion*
> *With the choices that you have made to be here*
> *At this time in your own unfolding history*
> *Which is the mystery of life*
> *And the unfolding that lasts forever*

As I listened with the inner ear to these whispers of the Spirit within, how sweet it was to respond to its soul-seducing invitation to "Remember, remember your True Self, the Self that existed even before you took human incarnation, even before your parents were born." It is the haunting call of the I AM that announces itself within us, that walks through our feet, breathes through our breath, beats in our heart. It is That which individualized itself as me, as you. Why postpone for one moment longer the rapture of merging in oneness with this Reality? Enter your inner temple through the door of meditation and become entwined in this mystical cord that binds you in oneness with kosmic creation, tenderly pulling you toward remembering Who and What is traveling in, through, and as you.

As you sit in the temple of meditation, know that you are not alone. All the saints, sages, bodhisattvas, and enlightened ones are cheering you on. As the mind and five senses calm themselves, space is created for the realization that you are sitting on the lap of Infinitude, that you are held in an embrace of unconditional love and grace. No matter what arises, whether it's thoughts of how well your meditation it's going, how bored you are, sensual thoughts, "good" thoughts, or egotistical thoughts, know such discursiveness is not part of your true self. The Self doesn't think—it is self-knowing. Any quality, habit, or pattern of thinking that can be dropped is because it is not part of your essential nature. You are the Witnessing Self, that which is left when ego disappears. Jump, throw yourself with abandon into this inner sky, which is Love.

As you begin to be conscious now that your body is breathing
And that it needs no help from you at this moment
As you now begin to be conscious that your heart is beating
And that you're lengthening that cord of memory
And becoming more aware that it needs no help from you
That there is something about you that is of life and of beauty
And of eternity
And you? You're remembering
You're on a journey that never ends
And is always beginning
A journey of discovery, a journey of realization
A journey of uncovering more that is within you
And then setting it free

You have never been born and never will die. Enjoy this kosmic movie. You are on a journey which takes you into the ever-new, ever-expansive terrain of your own infinite nature. Once you grow deep roots into your being, you will express your individuality beyond the desperate strivings of the ego. You will catch which qualities you are meant to cultivate and deliver on the planet and how to express your uniqueness, even as you discover the ordinariness of being an enlightened being. Ordinary, I say, because enlightenment is our naturally occurring, organic state of being, regardless of appearances to the contrary.

Too often we suffer because of our preconceived notions of how an awakened being should look, behave, speak, and walk in the world. We cannot imagine ourselves being among them when we consider our personality characteristics and quirks. This is the time to treasure the preciousness of the Self, to remind ourselves that Spirit so respects and trusts our awakening process that its Life Force sustains and nurtures us no matter how many lifetimes it takes for us to become self-realized.

How precious and practical it is to devote your energies to this unfolding of your soul, to ultimate attunement with your divine destiny. With loving kindness and compassion toward yourself, patiently yet with potent intent, consciously lengthen the mystic cord of memory. Surrender into the arms of the Divine as comfortably and trustingly as you would to a cherished lover, a devoted mother, a true friend.

Yes, I invite you to relax and remember this
And in so doing we allow the dust and grit
Of the journey of forgetting to be wiped away
That we can remember once again
That there's nothing wrong with us
That there's nothing missing in us
That everything is for us
And that there is nothing against us

Drop the myth of perfection, for it is a trickster, an obstacle on the path. Having taken a human incarnation, you cannot avoid being buffeted by the turbulence of the collective human experience, which means at times you stand in the face of stagnation, doubt, worry, lack, limitation, fear of change, loss, the impermanence of it all. When these human emotions drop in for tea and we imbibe a taste of amnesia, it is the perfect time to lengthen the mystic cord of memory and remind ourselves of their emptiness, that they have no substance. It is the time to pull up our sense of humor about this monolithic sense of "me" and remember the I AM that is our true nature. Surrender. Relax into Spirit's embrace. Hear its tender whisper, "All is well my beloved, all is well." Ah, how spiritually delicious is this communion with the Self.

Let us remember this together
So that the angst and the dread and the burden
And the worry can be wiped clean in this moment
And that we can awaken moment by moment
With such enthusiasm for life
Such enthusiasm for this grand, unfolding discovery of good
Relax into the awareness
That everything we could want, hope for, and desire
It's already been given
And we get to explore it
We get to discover it

We get to activate it
And yes, we get to express it

What we label as our burdens and challenges evaporate when we realize that the Spirit's treasure house has always been and always will be open to us. Too humble to force itself upon us, with tender patience it has awaited the day when we enter and claim our divine inheritance. Exploring its vast caverns, we discover wondrous, unimaginable beauty; creativity; intelligence; love; and bliss. The address of this treasure house is our innermost being where our godliness, our eternality lives, where every human yearning is dissolved in the intoxicating recognition of our true Self. The Master Alchemist, merging all seeming opposites within us, delights as we dance ecstatically in its Light, our inherent innocence smiling back at us through its radiance.

In these moments we give up the struggle of tinkering with ourselves, we drop our anxiety about our human imperfections, because we have tasted the essence of our beingness as Hafiz describes, "…though only once of late did I get so close to see my own face and heart reflected in Your wondrous soft eyes."

Relax, relax, relax now
The Universe is in order
All is well

Give yourself permission
To let all be well in your world
Give yourself permission
To feel that everything is working together for your good
Give yourself permission
To feel that you have a right, a reason
And yes, even a mandate from Life itself to be here
To set these gifts, talents, powers, visions
To set them free

Accepting that there are occurrences in life that ego's efforts cannot control gives us permission to relax, to surrender. Whether we're meditating, praying, exercising, blending a smoothie, attending a class, working, feeding our dog—it's all part of our journey to awakening, it's all an aspect of our spiritual practice. The point is that we fully open ourselves to our path and receive the gifts it has to offer. There are times when our journey goes smoothly, when our talents and skills are recognized and appreciated, while at other times we ride into old ruts and over bumps of habits that sabotage our best intentions. Under both conditions something kicks in that is bigger than we are and makes our journey delightful, interesting, easier to tread. That something is Grace.

Grace tells us that we are not alone, that we are always accompanied, that everything, no matter what label we put on it, is working together for our greater good. When we can't find the light and then suddenly we do, that is the grace of the Creator Life within us. There is every reason to not hold on so tightly, to relax in the midst of our vigilant commitment to grow, develop, and unfold, to give ourselves permission to invite this Grace to point us in new directions, new horizons. In a state of relaxation, Life begins to caress you.

The body's breathing, the heart is beating
The lungs are extracting oxygen
With no conscious help from you right now
As you notice that the body is breathing
Notice that the dust and grit of anxiety and fear
They're dissolving
Anxiety and fear are unraveling
Anxiety and fear, they're being transmuted
Those thought forms that emerged
From a sense of resistance and separation
They're dissolving now
Transmuting from this higher awareness
That there's nothing against you and that everything is for you
They're dissolving

Anxiety and fear cannot maintain their grip on you. They are aliens to your true nature, and have no permanent home in you. That is why they can be dissolved. Any emotion, thought, or action that you can separate from yourself is because it is not a component of your true nature. There is no need to resist false enemies. Drop your weapon of self-judgment. Toss away your ego's protective armor and laugh.

We cannot laugh genuinely and still hold on to fear and anxiety. Let your belly and shoulders shake with laughter. Have the courage to see yourself through and through, and fall in love with what you see, for that is the Creator Life individualized as you. Relax into your being, and trust in your potential to become a completely enlightened being.

> *It's okay to feel this*
> *I want you to give yourself permission to feel this*
> *You have authority*
> *You are your own authority*
> *Give yourself permission to feel this now*
> *Simply say, "I give myself permission to fly in the realm of peace*
> *In the realm of joy, to fly in the realm of knowing*
> *That all of my needs are met*
> *I give myself permission to know*
> *That I am cradled in such good and such beauty*

I give myself permission to be free
I relax in this permission
I rejoice, I sing, I fly, I flow
I relax in this dynamic good
That by means of me wants to express itself
My body temple, my mental body, my emotional body
The body of my affairs
I now give myself permission
To allow these bodies to reflect and to reveal
The order of the cosmos"

Release struggling against yourself or circumstances. Be comforted by the openness of your own heart. Life is really a dance when the world is viewed with clear seeing. Then the Whole can freely flow through your loving, through your everything. This upsurge of energy comes from within when you pull on the mystic cord of memory, reminding you of your inherent glory, goodness, and empowerment. There is no moment more spiritual than the one we are in.

"Now" is always happening. This is the main point: If you allow more life to flow through you, then more life happens. Goodness is embedded in your neurons. Nothing can diminish or destroy it. Trust the fundamental goodness of the universe and within yourself. Trust brings relaxation.

Say to yourself, "It's happening right now
I now can let go, I can relax into it
I can let it be as I flow
In this endless journey whose destination is
More light and more love and more beauty
And more joy and more abundance
And more creativity expressing through and as me
I say to myself
I let the healing happen"

Say it to yourself
"I let the Wholeness emerge
I let the creativity flourish
I let the abundance reveal itself in my life
I let the plenitude express itself in my life
I let the order of the kosmos order my steps
All is well now"

Your being is pure "is-ness." Understanding this, you have grasped the meaning of life. The truth points to this: that we are godly by nature. Our work is to uncover this truth within us. Challenges we encounter in the process aren't hang-ups; they are creative opportunities to go deeper into our inner core and invite greater creativity, love, joy—all the qualities of our soul—to flow through us, to circulate and share them with the world. Let acceptance be your prayer, let declarations of wholeness be your prayer. Claim your inner inheritance in this now moment. Relax into a state of receptivity, into acceptance that Existence is caressing you. Life is showering its gifts of love, beauty, abundance, creativeness on you. Take a posture of power, breathe into your heart, and be bathed in its purifying waters.

Now say to yourself, "I am guided, I am guarded
And I am directed by a living intelligence
In which I am living, moving, and having my Being
Even now"

Stretch the mystic cord of memory into remembrance of your intrinsic beauty, your lovability. Trust that you are guided, guarded, supported all along the way. Let Love-Intelligence determine the course of your life, trusting where it leads you. Know beyond any doubt that there is never a time, not even in your most seemingly desolate moments, that you are separate from divine love, from the infinite tenderness of Spirit, from its sublime intimacy with your soul.

Let yourself lengthen the mystic cord of memory
Let yourself remember again that life is for you and not against you
Let yourself remember once again
That you're on a sweet and wonderful journey
This journey in which you are now coming back to yourself

Remember you're coming to yourself
Remember, come back to yourself, your real self
Your essential self, your authentic self, original self
Remember this sweet and wonderful journey beckons you
And is a mandate from Life itself
Yield to this, relax into this, say yes to this
Feel your whole being say
"I let the order of the cosmos order my steps
all is well now."

And so it is.

You are made from the essence of Essence. Its effulgence is the cause of the fire in your heart to know your true nature. Turn your gaze within and return to yourself. Surrender yourself to your Self, for this is the root of all yearning, to go homeward within and find there the fulfillment of all desiring. Nothing in the external world compares to our inner riches. If ever there has been a well-kept secret, it is that we are already enlightened beings and the spiritual path is simply for the purpose of entwining ourselves in the mystic cord of memory and getting free of all that would bind us to ignorance of our awakened self.

Remember that you are a spiritual being having a human incarnation. Stretch the mystic cord of memory, and reveal the all-ness that is you in human form. The universe is one big love affair, kosmic creation in love with all that exists. Separation is an illusion; oneness is Reality. Again and again, devote and re-devote yourself to taking hold of the mystic cord of memory until it becomes completely unwound, leaving you gazing into your original face, which is the face of the Beloved.

"Once you hear the Truth, it's not going to rest Until it becomes fully available in your awareness."

Michael Bernard Beckwith is the Founder & Spiritual
Director of Agape International Spiritual Center in
Los Angeles, a transdenominational, multicultural
community where music holds a significant place in the
weekly celebrations, classes, and conferences. He is
also an award-winning author and internationally renowned
spiritual teacher who appeared in his own PBS Special,
The Answer Is You; has been a guest on *The Oprah Winfrey
Show, Larry King Live, 20/20,* and *Tavis Smiley;* and was
featured in *The Secret.*

Beckwith is also Co-founder and President of the Association
for Global New Thought (AGNT); convener of the Synthesis
Dialogues with His Holiness the Dalai Lama; and a teacher
of meditation, life visioning, and affirmative prayer.

Together with his wife, Rickie Byars Beckwith, "The Rev"
(as he is known to friends and Agape community members)
has written over 200 songs that have been recorded and
performed worldwide.

With *TranscenDance Expanded,* Michael Bernard Beckwith
invites you to shapeshift your life through powerful teachings
and ecstatic grooves. Dance floor not included.

For more information regarding Agape International Spiritual Center
in Los Angeles, visit www.agapelive.com

Stay Connected! Stay Expanded.

Hear Michael Bernard Beckwith on
Hay House Radio

THE ANSWER IS YOU – Pulled By A Vision
Every Weds. at 10AM Pacific Time
www.hayhouseradio.com

AGAPE MEDIA WISDOM CIRCLE
www.AgapeMe.com
Sign up and receive free downloads, monthly
specials and 10% off selected AMI offers.

FACEBOOK
www.facebook.com/michael.b.beckwith

TWITTER
www.twitter.com/drmichaelbb

MOBLI
www.mobli.com/therev

PBS SPECIAL | The Answer Is You
www.AgapeMe.com/TheAnswerIsYou

AGAPE LOVE STREAMERS | www.agapelive.com
Live Streaming of Agape services every Sunday
morning (6:30am, 8:30am & 11am)
and Wednesday evening (6:45pm).

AGAPE ONLINE COMMUNITY
http://agapelive.iamplify.com/
Join a global community based on unity,
wisdom, spirituality, and love. Receive weekly
audio downloads and monthly teleconference
calls with Michael Bernard Beckwith.
Subscribe now and receive two months free.

WAKE UP – The Sound of Transformation
KPFK 90.7 FM - Pacifica Radio | Los Angeles
and online at KPFK.org
Every Friday 1:00PM Pacific Time
Michael Bernard Beckwith with dynamic guests
such as Wayne Dyer, Alanis Morissette and others.

RICKIE BYARS BECKWITH
www.rickiebb.com

AGAPE MEDIA YOUTUBE CHANNEL
www.youtube.com/agapemedia

TRANSCENDANCE WEBSITE
www.BeckwithTranscenDance.com

OTHER OFFERINGS from Agape Media Artists & Authors

Agape Media International (AMI) is dedicated to promoting artists and art forms that uplift the human spirit and inspiring individuals to contribute their own talents to the creation of a world that works for everyone.

BOOKS

Michael Bernard Beckwith | The Answer Is You
  —Heart-Sets & Mind-Sets for Self-Discovery
Michael Bernard Beckwith | 40-Day Mind Fast Soul Feast
Michael Bernard Beckwith | Life Visioning
  —A Transformative Process for Activating Your Unique Gifts and Highest Potential
Michael Bernard Beckwith | Spiritual Liberation
  —Fulfilling Your Soul's Potential
Dianne Burnett | The Road to Reality*—Voted Off the Island!...My Journey*
  as a Real-Life Survivor
Charles Holt | Intuitive Rebel*—Tuning In to the Voice That Matters*
Cynthia Occelli | Resurrecting Venus*—Embrace Your Feminine Power*
Carl Studna | Click!*—Choosing Love One Frame at a Time*

AUDIO PROGRAMS & AUDIO BOOKS
by Michael Bernard Beckwith

Life Visioning (6-CDs)
The Life Visioning Process (2-CDs)
Life Visioning Kit (2-CDs, Workbook & Cards)
The Rhythm of a Descended Master
Your Soul's Evolution
Living From the Overflow
Spiritual Liberation Audio Book
Life Visioning Audio Book

DVDs

The Answer Is You-PBS Special
Spiritual Liberation, the Movie
Superwise Me!–*The Law of the Heart*
Living In The Revelation

MUSIC CDs

Music From The PBS Special–The Answer Is You
   feat. Will.I.Am, Siedah Garrett, Niki Haris, Rickie Byars Beckwith,
   Agape International Choir
Jami Lula & Spirit in the House / There's a Healin' Goin' On
Charles Holt I I Am
Charles Holt I Rushing Over Me
Rickie Byars Beckwith I Supreme Inspiration
Ester Nicholson I Child Above the Sun
Ben Dowling I The Path of Peace
Michael Bernard Beckwith / TranscenDance

CARDS

Life Lift-Off Cards

www.agapeme.com